AF825078

# INFORMATIONCOMMUNICATION TECHNOLOGY AND EDUCATION

# INFORMATION COMMUNICATION TECHNOLOGY AND EDUCATION

*(In 5 Volumes)*

**Framework for ICTs and Teacher Education**

**(Volume 4)**

V. C. PANDEY

© **Author**
All rights reserved. No part of this work may be reproduced, stored, adapted, or transmitted in any form or by any means, electronic, mechanical, photocopying, micro-filming, recording or otherwise, or translated in any language, without the prior written permission of the copyright owner and the publisher. The book is sold subject to the condition that it shall not, by way of trade or otherwise, be lent, resold, hired out, or otherwise circulated without the prior publisher's written consent in any form of binding or cover other than that in which it is published.

The views and opinions expressed in this book are author(s) own and the facts reported by them have been verified to the extent possible, and the publishers are not in any way liable for the same.

ISBN : 978-81-8205-xxx-x (Set)
ISBN : 978-81-8205-xxx-x
First Published in 2018
*Published by*
Isha Books
D-69, New Gupta Colony,
Near DDA Market
Delhi — 110009
Ph.: +91-9212142040

# Preface

Information and communication technology (ICT) is a major factor in shaping the new global economy and producing rapid changes in society. Within the past decade, the new ICT tools have fundamentally changed the way people communicate and do business. They have produced significant transformations in industry, agriculture, medicine, business, engineering and other fields. They also have the potential to transform the nature of education, where and how learning takes place, and the roles of students and teachers in the learning process.

The new technologies challenge conventional conceptions of both teaching and learning methods and materials and, by reconfiguring how teachers and learners gain access to knowledge, have radical implications for conventional teaching and learning processes. To meet these challenges, schools must embrace the new technologies and appropriate the new ICT tools for learning. They must also move toward transforming the traditional paradigm of learning.

There has been alarmingly little progress with respect to ICT and the progress has been quite makeshift.

Teacher training institutions are going in the right direction but they lack the quality, expertise, intensity, attention, momentum, etc. The shortage of expertise is not so much in basic digital skills, but in the educational use of ICT. The structure and content of teacher training programmes on ICT in education are underdeveloped.

Teacher education institutions may either assume a leadership role in the transformation of education or be left behind in the swirl of rapid technological change. For education to reap the full benefits of ICT in learning, it is essential that preservice and inservice teachers are able to effectively use these new tools for learning. Teacher education institutions and programs must provide the leadership for preservice and inservice teachers and model the new pedagogies and tools for learning. They must also provide leadership in determining how the new technologies can best be used in the context of the culture, needs and economic conditions within their country.

The book explores the radical implications of ICT for conventional teaching and learning processes. It discusses the challenges for ICT in teacher education and gives guidlines to the new generation of teachers as well as existing teachers, how to be well-prepared to use the new tools and pedagogies for learning.

*Editor*

# Contents

# 1

# Effective Use of ICTs in Education

The last 20 years have seen some remarkable innovations in the delivery of education. Nevertheless, many would argue that, as remarkable as these innovations are, they are no more than a beginning. The technologies available today, and those about to emerge, have the potential to transform the business of education. However, what may be impeding that potential is academic culture and traditions. Nine centuries of organized education have generated strong views and deep-seated beliefs about what is best and what is not.

The role of ICTs in the context of the global opportunities and challenges confronting the design, delivery, and administration of education to meet the diverse needs, clients, demands, goals, and objectives of nations and communities-particularly during a period of transition of societies and economies from an industrial base to one that is knowledge—and information-centered.

Some nations may decide to invest in technology for education for the 'glitz factor': the technology is there; it is fashionable to have the latest and the best, and it gives a sense of progress to use state-of-art-technology. This can be described as the technology for its own sake rationale. Other nations may base their investment decisions on the genuine case for improving the efficiency of their education systems or for some other benefits intrinsic to education. For instance, databases and computerized records in education systems have clear advantages and benefits. This is the 'technology for educational benefits' rationale. A third rationale may be external to education and concerned with developing skills for the labour market. A different view of the use of ICTs is Bill Gates's, who says:

> Students can look at their grades and even turn in their homework over the Web. Teachers hold online discussion groups. Students e-mail friends and family as naturally as they call them. Students are the ultimate knowledge workers. Their 'job' is to learn and explore and find unexpected relationships between things.

In between cynicism and optimism, one government took the view that it is fully committed to ensuring that all schools and teachers are in a position to deploy new information and communication technologies [ICTs] to raise educational standards to enhance learning and to prepare young people with the ICT skills they will need in society and at work in the twenty-first century.

The demand for more open and accessible learning has continued to increase since the early 1950s, but even more so following the World Conference on Education for All in Jomtien, Thailand, in 1989. Many factors are contributing to this changing educational culture, the most important of which are economic, social, and technological forces. These forces are worldwide in scope and power, and have had a profound impact on business practices, manufacturing processes, financial services, government policies, and, more recently, teaching practices and learning behaviors. It would not be an exaggeration to say that as embark on a new century, also moving irrevocably in the direction of changing the way about information, knowledge, and learning. Individuals and governments are beginning to recognize that planning for 'competitive advantage' will require a labour force that has literacy and numeracy skills beyond three to six years of primary schooling (the current situation in most industrialized and newly industrializing countries, and even grimmer in developing nations).

Globally, some 2 billion people who are in today's workforce will continue to be there well into the first quarter of this century. Their knowledge and skills will need continuous renewal. Added to this, 1 billion more young children and adults who will require initial education and training. The level of supply (or lack) of education and training for this huge demand for initial.

The challenge of providing education and training to a huge and diverse population with a variety of learning goals and styles, at an acceptable cost, will require new forms of global educational delivery. Notwithstanding the skepticism of many in the academic community. In some ways, the emergence of new technologies may have something to do with the push to make drastic changes in the nature of the learning environment. There is also a change in the nature of those requiring education and training. Communities no longer are content (nor should they be) to limit access to education and training to the fortunate few who are able; literate; live in urban communities; have access to communications, infrastructure, and classrooms; are knowledgeable about learning opportunities and options; and have the resources to pay for them. A fairer, kinder, and more concerned humanity requires that the education provide must be made available to a broader range of historically underserved groups, including:

— *Functional illiterates:* Apart from about 900 million illiterates globally, there are almost half as many adults who cannot cope with the demands of daily life because they lack literacy.

— *Physically disabled:* Annually, in Asia alone, about 15 million people become disabled as a result of war, diseases, accidents, and malnutrition. Their major hope for self-improvement lies in obtaining needed skills.

— *Long-term unemployed:* Long-term unemployment is a debilitating pathology; training people in such situations poses special challenges to delivery and pedagogy.

— *Out-of-work youth, especially boys:* This group is highly vulnerable to socially disruptive behaviors. Youth need vocational training, including apprenticeship and self-education, to be part of a productive economy.

— *Women and girls:* In many parts of the world, women and girls still find themselves marginalized in education and training; ways may have to be found to circumvent the social, cultural, and economic impediments they face.

— *Refugees, recent immigrants:* Today, roughly 125 million people live outside their countries of origin, and this number is ever increasing. This flow of people for political, social, or economic purposes is not expected to slow down. To help these people resettle, educational programs, language teaching, and training for social and job skills must be designed and delivered.

In contrast with this escalating demand is the lack of preparedness of a vast majority of education systems to deal even with existing demand, under circumstances that, in the words of one activist group, 'violate the rights of children' through 'dilapidated schools, inadequate facilities, poorly trained and under trained teachers, inadequate supplies of learning materials, irrelevant curricula, disregard for minority cultures and languages, gender bias and instructional methods which undermine, rather than nourish the potential of children.'

World over, the arrival of newer technologies certainly seems to have stimulated a resurgence of interest in diversifying methods of knowledge delivery. Almost daily, yet another Web-based course becomes available from one university or another. Smart schools are springing all over the richer world, and virtual learning, online learning, and other, newer forms of educational delivery are becoming part of the educational jargon of the new century.

Even before the arrival of the newer technologies, institutions such as the Correspondence School of New Zealand; the National Open School of India; the Open Universities of Sri Lanka, Hong Kong, and the UKOU; and the Indira Gandhi National Open University of India were providing good-quality, mass, flexible, and lower-cost education for remote learners from basic to university-level education using the older analog technologies of print, audio, video, and radio and television.

The experience and successes of these institutions around the world are testimony to the effectiveness of technologies to reach individuals and large communities simultaneously. They have transformed the delivery of education and, in the process, also transformed the business of education. In addition, full-time study within the timetabled constraints of the classrooms is only accessible to a few; for many who wish to study, learning has to occur at a time and place of their choice. The growth of open schools, polytechnics, and universities, as well as the numerous suppliers of correspondence and online education, are all manifestations of peoples' desire to learn at their own convenience rather than at an institution's call.

Information Explosion estimated that the total amount of information doubles every four to five years. Stated in another way, the total of information available to an undergraduate in 1997 was less than 1% of what will be available to a student in 2050. Teachers have to become expert in helping learners to navigate through this sea of information rather than attempt to be effective transformers of that information into knowledge for the learners. Students must be trained to bring about this transformation, during and beyond the school years. ICTs are crucial in coping with the explosion of knowledge over the lifetime of the learner; otherwise, peoples knowledge becomes obsolete, and countries become marginalized.

To function effectively in the modern world, citizens need more than a basic education. The structure and content of learning activities should equip all children, youth, and adults with the knowledge, skills, values, and attitudes they need to survive, to improve their quality of life, to empower them to participate fully and responsibly in the life of their communities and nations. This education also should help them to initiate and adapt to the changing circumstances of their environment, and to continue learning according to their individual needs and interests. Clearly, any strategy to engage all citizens in lifelong learning will require application of technologies, especially mass media. For the first time in the history of humankind, communication technologies enable us to reach millions of people across continents simultaneously.

At the same time, variations of these modern technologies allow educators to tailor content to suit a narrow local audience to respond to individual learning needs. Satellite, community, and Internet-based (through telecenters) delivery of content all enrich the environment for learning. Agriculture, farming, health, market conditions, maternal care, and reproductive sciences all being delivered today through ICTs. Local community radio and telecenter facilities are extremely versatile tools and are used effectively and imaginatively around the world today.

A key feature of the modern global society is the primacy associated with the exchange over computer-communication networks of intangibles such as knowledge, ideas and intelligence, rather than tangible goods that have long been the basis of human interaction. It is also becoming fairly clear that the power of the computer chip will continue to increase while the cost of building it decreases; bandwidths will broaden and convergence heighten; and the penetration of the Internet will continue to rise while the lack of connectivity drops.

Acquisition of up-to-date knowledge, skills, and education will determine the success of individuals and democratic societies both economically and socially. It is not surprising, therefore, that an ever-increasing number of countries wish to see their citizens technologically literate. From 'telecenters' to 'smart schools' the push to make every child computer-, Internet-, and Web-savvy has fast become an overriding concern for education ministers of developed and developing countries.

Despite the knowledge explosion and advances in information and technologies, in many countries, there are significant numbers of people who cannot read, let alone enjoy the benefits of a technological society. Every country in the world has committed to decreasing drastically the number of illiterate citizens.

Mass media, especially print, radio, and, to a certain extent, television, has played a significant role in adult literacy programs. In some parts of the world, newer technologies have been applied, albeit in a modest way. An increase in the use of ICTs seems to be constrained by financial resources, shortage of literacy workers skilled in using technologies, and lack of technical support for a well-functioning technology environment. However, ongoing developments using online resources to train literacy workers and create literacy products seem to demonstrate significant results. ICTs have the potential to:

— reduce the isolation many adult literacy providers and students experience;

— facilitate communication among staff and students within and between programs;

— increase access to high-quality materials and emerging research;

— streamline administrative and reporting processes; and

— help to provide the delivery vehicle for innovative instructional and staff development approaches.

On one hand, the planet is filled with highly skilled and talented people in all fields of human endeavour. On the other, critics of global educational systems constantly bemoan the fact that, by and large, the academic talent needed in schools, colleges, and universities to enhance the quality of the learning environment beyond perceived levels of mediocrity is in short supply.

The Western Governors Virtual University initiative among the northwestern states in the United States is in fact an attempt to do this. This attempt envisages going beyond campus walls to obtain academic 'teaching' talent. Contributors to courses will come from business, commerce, industry, and government, and those who take the courses will include ordinary people, along with thousands of college and university students.

Planning for effective use of ICTs in education necessitates understanding the potential of technology to meet different educational objectives and, consequently, deciding which of these objectives to pursue. This decision affects the choice of technologies and the modalities of use. There were four objectives that may be enhanced by ICTs:

— expanding access to all levels of education;
— improving the quality of education;
— enhancing lifelong learning; and
— facilitating nonformal education.

## Access for All Levels of Education

In most developing countries, full-time study within the time constraints of classrooms is only accessible to a few; for many who wish to study, learning will have to take place at a time and location of their choice. In addition, access to learning for those living in remote areas and those who are marginalized, isolated, or disadvantaged has to be sought vigorously as nations respond to the declaration made at Dakar in 2000. Either synchronously or asynchronously, barriers such as time, distance, and social and cultural constraints must be overcome. At the same time, rapid changes taking place in the workplace will require training to be delivered quickly. Such training must be high-speed, low-cost and capable of reaching small and large groups. As a policy consideration, the application of ICTs to enhance access to learning must receive the highest priority. ICTs in their many forms have been applied in a variety of contexts.

Provisions have to be made to reach, in particular, children in many parts of the developing world where formal schooling is likely to account for less than 1,000 days in their entire lifetime. Fewer than half of primary-school-age children actually are enrolled in school, and more than two-thirds of those who do manage to enter school fail to complete three years of schooling. While it will take a massive effort to change this situation, as an interim measure, ICTs can be employed in formal and informal settings to deliver essential knowledge and information.

The National Open School in India, using print, audio, local tutors, and ICT-based assessment and testing system on-call, provides postprimary eduction to remote villages throughout India. About 400,000 children have access to education up to grade-12 equivalence, and lessons prepared by teams of highly qualified teachers are made available to students free or at very low cost

## Gender Disparity in Educational Access

Gender disparity in educational access is a major challenge in many communities because of family and social circumstances. Inequalities between women and men extend from literacy classes to access to formal schooling and prospects for completing school. Social, cultural, religious, and economic factors all combine to create barriers and place girls and women at a serious disadvantage.

While such barriers will take time to remove, ICTs provide one way to circumvent them. Learning and training will have to find their way to girls and women where they are located, rather than expecting them to come to places where teaching is conducted. The Allama Iqubal Open University of Pakistan approached the challenge of illiteracy among women in Pakistan through a unique combination of print, audio, radio, and mentors.

Though all the technologies used were analog, the opportunity to digitize this effort and deliver it through local telelearning centers offers immense opportunities, in both qualitative and quantitative terms, to scale-up the effort. Increasingly, ICTs are being recognized and used to bring education and training to those individuals who are challenged in one way or another. These tools include digital voice control software, audio to visual conversions for the hearing impaired, electronic text, and digital audio. The technologies, either stand-alone or as part of integrated systems, help to overcome barriers such as instruction based only on print and dependent on sight, audio dependent on hearing, and video requiring vision. The systems themselves have to be developed for individual use, so they require careful study of individual students' needs.

Education of out-of-school youth, especially beyond the basic level, can benefit from the application of ICTs. Vocational and trade skills, competency-based training, and alternate entry paths to higher education can be achieved through creation of knowledge products for a variety of situations, from self-learning to flexible learning environments.

Multimedia commercial training products are becoming increasingly available for training in vocational skills. Governments can play an important role in enabling vocational training institutes, encouraging nongovernmental organizations (NGOs) engaged in supporting youth development, and prodding media outlets to use ICTs for youth training and personal development.

The National Open School (NOS) India was established in 1989 to support India's National Policy on Education. The school caters to the needs of school children as well as children from socially marginalized communities in both urban and rural locations. While the school's early focus was on academic programmes at the secondary school level, it currently offers courses in vocational and other life-skills areas. It also has extended its range from elementary to preuniversity programs. Some 400,000 children are enrolled, and they come from challenged communities, socially disadvantaged groups, and isolated populations. The school uses ICTs for course development, administration, testing, and to deliver some content by audio and local radio. Its plans for the future include even more extensive use of the newer technologies through tele- and community-learning centers.

## Environments for Open Learning

Smart schools, online education, and virtual universities are labels that have been attached to institutes applying a new set of strategies to deliver education using digital networks either synchronously or asynchronously. The technologies are used to deliver instruction, to manage the system's administrative services, and to provide support for learners. The last four decades have seen the emergence of colleges and universities dedicated to delivering tertiary-level education off-campus to learners, especially in those countries where the gap between the supply of and demand for tertiary-level education is huge and largely unmet. These universities apply open learning principles and distance education practices to deliver learning. They are generally universities with big student populations comprising mature and mostly part-time learners. Ten of the largest universities in the world are open universities, and all but one of them is located in developing countries. In total, they may have as many as 2 million students enrolled in their programs.

ICTs have always played an important role in managing and administering these universities, and older analog technologies such as radio and video also have been used to enrich the learning environment of the open universities. With the arrival of the newer digital technologies, ICTs also have begun to figure much more intensely in this role.

One of the most powerful reasons for considering using ICTs in an educational system is that they put learning in the hands of the user. They facilitate individualizing curriculum, permit learners to dictate the pace of learning, and widen sources of information. ICTs also promote active learning and allow for interaction between and among peers and mentors. Many would say as well that the quality and effectiveness of learning is enhanced many times through the use of ICTs. The technologies allow faculty to incorporate new information and update learning materials, and they enable immediate and rapid transfer of information pertaining to the administration of a course or program of study. Of these many educational objectives, the five below stand out as extremely important.

The Delors Commission report to UNESCO clearly and eloquently described the need to reform curriculum at all levels of education to prepare citizens for the new millennium. Learning to know, learning to do, learning to be, and learning to live together are all ideals that are achievable within the framework of basic and postbasic education. These recommendations recognize that today's learners, young and old, will spend their lives in a century that is information-rich, knowledge-dependent, and global. They need the skills to cope with this dynamic period. The growth of online library systems, easy access to expert knowledge through the Web, the variety of sources of learning, and frequent change of careers and location of residence during a person's productive lifetime will necessitate learning new skills and refreshing old skills. The curriculum should reflect these concerns and will include:

— The ability to frame problems when facing unfamiliar situations. Tomorrow's problems may be similar to yesterday's once they are well understood. But these present themselves in new forms. Once a problem has been framed, it must be solved and, often, both framing and solving problems will require powerful information technologies. Framing and solving problems sometimes will be simpler, but they often are likely to be more difficult than before.

— The ability to communicate, including with people from other groups. Nations' ethnic composition is becoming more diverse, and increasing globalization has meant having frequent contact with people of other nations and cultures. All of this requires sensitivity to numerous cultures, and some common and shared values and insights, if political and social tensions are to be avoided and conflicts minimized.

— The ability to work in, form, and lead teams and coalitions, including involving people of other cultures. This vital skill is seldom taught comprehensively in schools, and, as global interdependence increases in importance, so, too, does collaboration.

— The ability to identify what needs to be learned, and then learn it efficiently. ICTs often will furnish the means for learning. Every educated person will need to spend a certain fraction of his or her life keeping up with changes in that technology.

In all these areas, ICTs are an extremely invaluable asset. The Web, more than any other tool has the power to make enormous amounts of information from their original source available at the click of a button. This information, in its multimedia form, provides teachers and learners with information to support and enrich curriculum in the modern classroom. Subscriptions to digital libraries, collaborative programmes with peers outside of one's own classroom, and access to remote knowledge and expertise make lessons richer in content and, in the process, learning more exciting.

The time-driven, rigid organizational structures of institutions of learning, assumptions of learning, and traditions of teaching, as well as the urban location of teaching institutions, have combined to present barriers of one kind or another to learning for all but a small proportion of citizens.

The new ICTs provide enormous flexibility of use unlike older technologies, which required learners to be assembled in a controlled environment at a specific time and location. Radio and television had to be tied rigidly to schedules developed centrally. On the other hand, the new technologies are available for use 'anytime, anywhere.' The emergence of virtual education is very much a reflection of this versatility: Learners can access their education or training at the workplace, home, library, or anywhere connection to a telephone and power supply is available.

Learning technologies can affect education in systemic and structural ways. The challenge for educators is to bring about a balance among content learning, technology learning, and social experience. This balance depends on instructional strategies that accommodate individual learning styles and, at the same time, provide for effective assessment. Successful introduction of ICTs into the learning environment also includes support for interdisciplinary interaction with peers and instructors and among groups. This arrangement allows learners to interact with their institutions and their communities.

The newer technologies can change the relationship between teachers and learners to improve the learning process and learning experience. Traditional teaching and learning habits always have favored a certain passivity. Professors lectured and students listened and took notes; sometimes they asked questions, but they seldom contributed to knowledge. That was also true for the older technologies of print, radio, and television, despite the hype given them. Though active and independent learning were aspired to, they were hard to achieve, given the limitation of the technology.

New ICTs make it possible for students to be active learners. Both teachers and students can control, manipulate, and contribute to information and knowledge generation. Using ICTs, students not only make choices about the pace and order of a presentation, but also may choose topics for explorations; take notes; answer questions; explore virtual landscapes; simulate experiments; enter, draw, or chart data; create and manipulate images; make their own PowerPoint presentations; and communicate with others. ICTs have great capacity to facilitate the educational transaction between providers and users. For instance, ICTs can be used to:

— Keep students well informed about the courses that are available to them.

— Enhance teacher-learner contact, an essential part of a good educational environment, through e-mail, chat sessions, etc.

— Encourage active learning. Students do not learn much from memorizing facts and reproducing set answers; they derive greater benefits by being active in their learning.

- Facilitate peer support in learning. Sharing one's ideas and responding to the ideas of others improves thinking and increases understanding. Learning can improve if it is a team effort rather than a collection of solo performances.
- Provide immediate feedback and encouragement.
- Encourage paced learning through tools such as assignments, tutorials, broadcast programs, computers, conferencing, etc.
- Allow for effective mapping of learning pathways, which facilitate different styles of learning.

Like all other professions, teachers need constant and continuous renewal to be effective, motivated, and up to date in their knowledge and skills. While this is not a mandatory requirement in many national jurisdictions, those that do have such requirements use and see ICTs as important vehicles to provide continuing professional development to teachers. The use of ICTs, especially in support of distance education activities, adds enormous value to the training. Where the infrastructure exists, and connectivity costs are subsidized, the opportunity to create virtual online learning communities of teachers within nations and across regions exists. Such learning communities enable and empower trainee and practicing teachers to share experience, curriculum, learning materials, lesson notes, and collaborative programmes. ICTs can be applied in at least three training contexts:

- Basic training, upgrading and advancing pedagogical skills and content knowledge, and continuous professional development.

*Resource sharing:* Shared knowledge through the wonderful medium of books, only a fraction of human knowledge actually is published. Until the arrival of the computer, sharing knowledge, an important basis of education, was more wishful than real. With ICTs, sharing knowledge resources is enhanced many times over. Putting information on the Web makes it available immediately to anyone in the world with a suitable connection.

Teachers can share lesson plans with their colleagues in their own jurisdictions and with those far removed from their jurisdictions. Students from all over the world can undertake joint programmes, exchange findings, analyze data collectively, and draw reasoned conclusions. Knowledge about and of interest to minority groups, languages, and interests can enjoy the same opportunity to publish and share.

Lifelong learning is a necessity in a world that changes and renews itself so rapidly. Such dynamism makes demands on individuals to update themselves constantly in the context of their workplace, social life, and participation in healthy and vibrant democracies. Two broad categories of individuals use lifelong learning opportunities. The first group refers to those who are underrepresented across a whole range of postbasic education and includes, among others, illiterate and neoliterate populations engaged in unskilled work; ethnic, marginalized, and minority groups; people with learning difficulties; and the physically challenged. These learners face such obstacles as lack of learning skills, confidence, money, counselling and advice, and personal support, and they require active intervention by the state, the business sector, and voluntary organizations. The second group refers to those who have had the benefit of some form of postbasic education but are not equipped to deal effectively with the technology-driven environment in which they find themselves. This group includes out-of-school youth, employees in workplaces, individuals with basic training, professionals needing continuing education, and older adults seeking personal enrichment. These people are expected to know their needs, but they face challenges such as inadequate supply of learning opportunities, inflexibility of learning systems, lack of money, and inadequate supply of information.

There is increasing evidence that ICTs are beginning to play an effective role in promoting lifelong learning. Supported by a greater bandwidth capacity, digital and interactive radio and television, and multimedia, pathways are extending the speed with which learning products can be delivered to learners over large catchment areas. However, to make this happen, some basic conditions need to be met, including regulatory frameworks, infrastructure, affordable cost structures, public access to multimedia facilities, skills training in ICT use and employer support, and institutional commitment of learning providers.

As shifts occur in economic activity, so does the need to "retool" the workforce in response. This applies as much to a rice farmer as it does to an ICT worker. To maintain and enhance the competitive advantage of their workforces, nations are beginning to give more attention to training or retraining people. In a world made up of some two billion workers who will require regular access to training where they are working, the role of ICTs becomes critical. In British Columbia (BC), Canada, for example, a program called SkillPlan does exactly that. The training facility was developed as a result of a partnership between the Open Learning Agency (OLA) of BC and the province's Construction Industries Unions. The OLA identified a computer-managed learning system that provided adult basic education courses aimed at those who had completed high school certification. Workers who need to improve their reading and writing skills can 'drop in' at the Agency's local centers and use the system when it suits them. The system keeps track of each individual's progress and enables learners to carry on where they left off the last time they were able to drop in. The training center is equipped with ICT appliances and connections such as telephones, fax, and online. Another example of a dynamic arrangement is the Queensland Open Learning Network

The rapid changes taking place in the workplace will require training to be delivered quickly. Such training needs to be highspeed, low-cost, and accessible to small and large groups. Traditional ways of delivering training are time-consuming, labour-intensive, socially disruptive, and expensive. Workers have to acquire new skills quickly and affordably. It becomes even more attractive if such training can be delivered at the trainees' workplace.

Also, adult learners require flexibility, and they have families, work commitments, and social obligations around which they have to fit their training. This simply means that, ideally, training has to be accessible anywhere, anytime. Just-in-time-training is especially relevant in the context of business and industrial training where there is a continuous need to respond quickly to demands from the work environment.

## Nonformal education

ICTs are being used to make information and knowledge

available in nonformal contexts. The demand for enrichment learning is on the rise, particularly in countries experiencing an increase in aging populations and in populations with more leisure time who want to use it in intellectual pursuits. These are learners for pleasure, and, for them, activities in a classroom are not the ideal solutions. ICTs offer a convenient solution, but only if the individual has the skills needed to use the appliances and navigate through the millions of Web pages and is able to pay for the cost of the digital connection. Besides structured learning for enrichment purposes, unstructured learning opportunities are increasingly available through zoos, museums, planetariums, research institutions, professional societies, interest groups, commercial companies, and national agencies, among others.

The knowledge to be gained can range from virtual tours of, for example, archeological sites to the epidemiology of HIV/AIDS. It is as possible to learn to cook exotic food as it is to design and make quilts. One can participate in a debate on the World Trade Organization organized by supporters or detractors or engage in a discussion with a Nobel laureate on rain forest exploitation.

All of these learning opportunities inform citizens, enrich their lives, enable them to share indigenous knowledge, and empower them to participate in functioning democracies. The British government, for example, plans to connect all of the country's libraries to the Internet through a National Grid for Learning. In theory, this will allow citizens to browse through holdings throughout the country, a service that is especially valuable to those who are homebound.

Strategic planning for inclusion of ICTs in a nation's or institutions educational system is likely to be based on a number of perceptions, such as:

— acceptance of a learner-centered educational approach that involves the use of multimedia resources for self-paced, self-directed, flexible learning;

— acceptance that the role of teachers is changing from transmitters of knowledge to mediators in learning from a variety of information sources;

— the belief that systems that include technology can improve efficiency and/or effectiveness of student learning; and

— a perception of accelerated growth in demand among stakeholders for access to technology coupled with a rise in availability and use of ICTs elsewhere in society.

Strategic planning questions about the use of ICTs in education invariably will include a need to recognize the competing interests of stakeholders. It will be particularly important to align the learning technology strategy with strategy planned for related areas such as libraries and information systems, academic management (student records, accreditation's, credit banks, etc.), student support systems, student administration, and electronic media.

Even as recently as 10 years ago, the choice of technologies for delivering education was somewhat limited, partly because they were expensive, analog stand-alones with limited versatility, and they required skilled technicians to create and deliver the product.

Radio and television are prime examples of the demand these technologies made on educational systems. Today the picture has changed almost completely.

Technology application in education no longer is limited by the versatility, convenience, cost, and potential of the technology but, rather, only by imagination in the way technology can be applied. Through integration, convergence, miniaturization, and intelligence, technologies have become friendly. The question is no longer whether technologies are useful in the teaching and learning environment but which technologies are best suited for a particular purpose.

Digitization of many information and communication technologies has made it possible to design, develop, deliver, manage, and assess the learning and training process. The new digital technologies are not single technologies; they are combinations of hardware and software, media, and delivery systems. They are evolving and converging rapidly, as seen in PCs, laptops, notebooks, and digital cameras that are both video and single-image; local area networking; the World Wide Web; CD-ROMs and DVDs; application software, such as word processing, spreadsheets, and simulations; e-mail; digital libraries; and computer-mediated conferencing, videoconferencing, and virtual reality. They also have a capacity to integrate with older analog technologies from print, and through audio and video, make it possible to retrieve information stored in older technologies and to develop synergies between the old and the new. There are excellent reviews of the older analog technologies, which still have tremendous value, especially in many developing countries and their educational systems.

There are several important aspects from older technologies in their integration of multimedia, convergence of communication and information technologies, interactivity, flexibility of use, and connectivity. Understanding these differences will help us to appreciate why the use of ICT in education is expected to grow.

ICTs for teaching and learning range from those that rely on ubiquitous low-cost technology, such as the stand-alone PC, to those deployed for specific purposes at higher cost, such as the electronic classroom. Decisions on the choice of technologies are subject to many considerations and constraints, ranging from constancy of power supply to availability of skilled technical and managerial support to maintaining the technological infrastructure. Some of the newer IC technologies are:

*E-mail:* Increasingly, e-mail is becoming the most widely used medium, ranging in function from exchange of gossip, to serious dialogue and collaborative research. It also has become an important supplement to classroom teaching. Bulletin board services extend the classroom beyond fixed timetables; listservs bring communities of learners together; and assignments and term papers are beginning to be channeled routinely through e-mail. On-campus education is being enriched by e-mail facilities, and off-campus education is made more personal and interactive.

In economically developed countries, e-mail is almost as common as the telephone. In many cases, connections are free of charge, appliances are provided at low or no cost, and training is available for neophyte users. In poor economies, e-mail has yet to make its presence felt throughout society, but is increasingly available at community service centers such as libraries, telelearning centers, and 'cyber cafes.'

*Presentational Software :* PowerPoint and similar programs are already commonplace among academics and other professionals. While a simple slide presentation requires little skill to develop, the increasing sophistication level of such a presentation requires higher-level training.

*World Wide Web:* Many on-campus instructors are beginning to use the Web to make their lecture notes available to students at any time. The Web also has the advantage of providing access to primary sources of information in most media (print, graphics, photographs, audio, and video) through streaming. This technology requires good organizational and pedagogical skills to profit from its enormous potential, and faculty training in its use will be essential. The Web to be a low-cost technology for several reasons: the existence of simple computer languages such as HTML and intermediary course authoring systems such as the WebCT and Blackboard; it uses the Internet as a transport vehicle that involves no direct charge for independent packets of information, and pricing is by volume and not by time or distance; the Web's ability to combine media, thereby increasing its range of applications; access to high-quality learning resources inexpensively; it allows asynchronous interpersonal communication through e-mail, bulletin boards, and discussion forums; and it enables cross-cultural, international, collaborative learning.

*Multimedia, CD-ROM, DVD:* Multimedia, CD-ROMs, and DVDs are very exciting learning tools. Their development costs can be very high, especially those at the very high end that can carry large quantities of data in a variety of formats, such as audio and video clips, Internet connections to other databases, large amounts of information, and built—in simulation and other enrichments. Putting all these together in user-friendly packages will require teams of experts, from media producers to content experts. The reproduction cost of CD-ROMs can be reduced considerably if large numbers are 'burned.' Consequently, this medium is a consideration only when enrollments are large enough to justify the development expense. However, there is a strong case for developing the medium when the course can be used by a consortium of institutions working together.

*Satellite Broadcasting* : Satellite broadcasting for educational purposes has a long history. Countries such as India and China, and such regional universities as the University of the West Indies and University of the South Pacific have long used satellites to deliver audio- and video-based lectures to all corners of their region. Satellites serve as good vehicles to carry lessons, and, by marrying satellites to ground facilities, it is possible to build a two-way learning environment. In addition, their digital technologies allow for further sophistication to be built into the learning systems. However, because of their high start-up cost, satellites' value for educators is limited. Recent developments sponsored by private enterprises such as World Space have combined satellite technologies with digital ones to broadcast voice and data directly to specially designed digital receivers over very large geographic areas. While this venture is driven by and for commercial interests, special provision for educational purposes allows educational providers to reach very remote and isolated parts of the world. World Space eventually expects to reach an audience of some three billion people. While satellite technology has some significant advantages in terms of reach and low unit cost, for it to be truly effective as a learning technology requires extensive local support on the ground, either on an interpersonal basis or through telephony, the Internet, etc. Ground support will cause costs to increase considerably, thereby reducing the economic benefits. Well designed printed texts can be more educationally cost-effective than real time or even recorded satellite lectures.

*Videoconferencing:* In the late 1970s, multicampus postsecondary institutions began experimenting with videoconferencing to distribute their education and training services and lectures in real time. With the decreasing costs of telephony, videoconferencing has become relatively popular, especially in Australia and the United States. This technology, an amalgam of telephony and computer-compressed technologies, reduces the amount of time instructors and students spend travelling from campus to campus to deliver and receive lessons. It also saves instructors from having to repeat lectures.

The traditional culture of classroom teaching is preserved, and no new skills have to be learned by students or teachers. It is not a flexible system of learning, however. New innovations incorporating videoconferencing technologies with the Internet and Web technologies offer new opportunities, notwithstanding some concerns about the visual and voice quality of such arrangements. Broadly speaking, ICTs can be used for either one of two purposes, or, in some cases, for both purposes simultaneously.

Enhance the richness and quality of education on-campus and in the classroom; distribute campus-developed knowledge products off-campus through distributed learning, distance education, and open flexible learning. In either case, the selection of technological tools will depend on costs, the technology infrastructure of the learning system, learner access to the technology, the support personnel and facilities available to create digitized knowledge products, and the institutional commitment to sustaining the venture.

Based on an extensive review of European universities, and embedded in a few assumptions relating to the use of technologies, the Association of European Universities-under the sponsorshipo f the European Union's Socrates program-developed a set of guidelines for using ICTs. Under the right conditions and used properly, the technologies can be highly effective as both teaching and learning tools. The challenge for institutions is to develop the knowledge and skills to exploit the technologies' full potential.

At the heart of all learning that uses ICTs are materials specially designed to exploit the full potential of the available technologies. These materials normally include content in the form of texts, special 'books of readings,' specially developed study or learner's guides, assignments and assessments pads, and instructor's or tutor's guides. These resources, along with appropriate learner support systems, complete the educational or training environment. There are two ways by which institutions acquire these learning and teaching resources: they design and develop them either by themselves or in partnership with like-minded collaborators, or they purchase, lease, or acquire-through other arrangements—materials already developed and adapt them for their unique needs.

Developing interactive multimedia learning materials is an exceedingly interesting challenge. They can be constructed from a combination of media, sometimes quite modest in cost and sophistication, such as a combination of computer- aided instruction (CAI) and print, and at other times very expensive and elaborate, using a combination of DVD, CD-ROM, hypermedia, and virtual reality. Miller compared the process of production to an orchestra in which each musician not only plays a different instrument, but also speaks a different language. Such is the case with interactive video, where the assembled team includes instructional designers who speak of authoring, pedagogics and remediation; graphic artists who talk of drop shadows, GUI's and animated sprites; video producers who think in terms of wipes, fades, pictures, plots, scenes and storylines; and computer specialists who deal in bits and bytes, images and data, icons, picons, microns and programming language all their own. Add to this a systems person who wants to integrate DVD's and CD-ROMS and Windows via SCSI or R232 ports, and then telecommunicate the whole mess to a host... Despite the complexities involved in the design and creation of multimedia materials, it is important to plan before developing and producing learning materials that integrate print, audio, and video into a seamless and fluid learning experience.

For well over three decades now, and long before the arrival of the newer technologies, dedicated distance teaching institutions such as the open universities of the UK, Canada, India, Thailand, Turkey, Israel, South Africa, and other countries have been developing courses using a variety of media. The experience gained through these institutions is just as relevant in today's technology-rich environment, where digitization allows for totally seamless integration, as it was then in an analog world.

Unlike face-to-face teaching, the design and development of interactive multimedia materials involves the knowledge, skills, and expertise of a number of individuals. Therefore, assembling a team to undertake the task is almost a prerequisite if a high-quality product is the ultimate objective. The size of the team, and the skills of the individuals who make up the team, will depend on the sophistication of the product to be developed. It is possible, though not advisable-as is often the case in many small operations-for one person to create the learning materials.

At a minimum, the course team should have a content expert and an instructional designer. In addition to content experts and instructional designers, complex course team composition may involve audio and video producers, editors, ICT specialists, publishers, and programme managers. The team approach will require a totally different work culture from what is normally associated with academe.

Digitization of knowledge products opens up unprecedented opportunities for their portability. CD-ROMS, DVDs, and other multimedia have the capacity to carry entire courses on a single disc. Furthermore, granulation of knowledge allows for greater manipulation of the content to suit particular needs and clients. There are also economies to be gained. However, acquiring knowledge products from other sources for local use requires careful consideration of many issues and factors, besides intellectual property rights and economic concerns; sometimes it is cheaper to produce courses in house than to purchase and adapt them.

Contextual—the cultural, learning, and teaching traditions and the location of learners require consideration. In cultures where traditions of learning and teaching are more didactic, enquiry-based approaches to learning may not be a suitable fit. This is especially so at lower levels of study. Also important is the tone and simplicity of the language used.

Disadvantaged learners-individuals from minority groups, as well as physically, aurally, and visually challenged individuals, may require special attention when materials are adapted for their purpose. Instructor skills-using the imported multimedia material skill of instructors has to be taken into account; provisions need to be made to train such teachers in new skills. Professional human assets-to enable local professionals to adapt the imported materials for local needs, all of the professional skills needed to create the original material need to be assembled and trained for purposes of adaptation.

Which policies and strategies for applying digital technologies to education and training must be considered. While there are enormous benefits to be gained in terms of quality, enrichment, and flexibility in using ICTs throughout formal educational systems, there is even greater value to be gained in using the technologies to increase access to millions of individuals who are currently outside the educational footprints of nations.

A combination of the newer and older technologies has the potential to overcome the barriers of time, distance, and inadequate prior learning facing all those who wish to be informed, educated, and trained. It is clear that ICTs offer opportunities not available previously to educators. Using tools such as e-mail; the Web; audio-, video-, computer-conferencing, both synchronously and asynchronously, a very rich interactive and individualized learning environment can be created that allows learners to dictate their pace of learning, place of learning, and the company they wish to keep (or not keep) while learning.

While the ICT tools empower the learner, they need not take away from the role of the instructor. Instead, communities of learners and instructors come together for a common purpose and on a shared platform. These communities can encompass all levels and sectors of learning, from basic education to postgraduate studies, from teacher training to business studies, and from nonformal studies to language instruction.

## Impact of ICT on Education

Social, economic, and technological changes of the past decades are making education and training for all more crucial than ever. Yet, educational systems, to different degrees worldwide, are struggling to afford educational opportunities for all, to provide their graduates with the necessary knowledge and skills for evolving marketplaces and sophisticated living environments, and to prepare citizens for lifelong learning. To meet these challenges, countries have to focus concurrently on expanding access, improving internal efficiency, promoting the quality of teaching and learning, and improving system management.

A linear expansion of existing processes and methods may not be sufficient to meet these objectives within a reasonable time. Some countries and institutions have turned to information and communication technologies (ICTs) and are exploring ways by which ICTs may help them in pursuing their educational goals. Frequently, users and experts tend to concentrate on what a specific technology can and cannot do for education.

But, as Table 1 illustrates, one technology may have different potentials depending on the purpose for using it. Also, many of the technologies have similar characteristics. Therefore assessments of the potential and appropriateness of particular technologies must be based on educational needs and objectives, rather than on the technologies themselves.

***Table 1: ICTs and their potential for education***

| *Technology* | *Outreach* | *Flexibility* | *Sensorial Stimulation* | *Interactivity* |
|---|---|---|---|---|
| Radio | High | Limited | Audio only | Limited |
| Television | High | Limited | Audio only | Limited |
| Video | Low | High | Audio only | Limited |
| PC | Low | High | Audio only | High |
| Internet | Highest | High | Audio only | Highest |

Expanding access to education is a matter of both economic development and social justice. It is true that worldwide illiteracy rates have declined in the past 30 years, but it is also true that the demands on knowledge are much higher now than 30 years ago. In the past, an agrarian society could thrive economically even when more than half of its population was barely literate, but this is no longer possible in modern societies in the Information Age. To remain economically competitive and prosper in this global, knowledge-driven economy, countries cannot afford to have large sectors of their population excluded from education, or at the lower level of the educational process.

Education is positively related to development-that is, a higher proportion of the population of the most developed countries has attained higher educational levels than the population of developing countries. In regions that have stronger economies, such as North America, Western Europe, and parts of Asia, more than half of the college-age youth population is indeed attending college. Tertiary enrollment in the least developed countries is about 3%.

Approximately 90 million secondary-school-aged children in Southern Asia were not in school in 2000, and in sub-Saharan Africa, the number of school-aged children who are not in school continues to grow. In many countries, whose budgets already are stretched thin, expanding access to education under traditional models is not an option. Dramatic conflicts and the burgeoning HIV/AIDS crisis (sometimes occurring simultaneously) in many countries have disrupted social services, including education, and diverted resources that could be used to maintain, let alone, expand educational opportunity. In Togo alone, public expenditure on education already represents 25% of total government expenditures. The country's illiteracy rate for youth aged 15-24 is close to 30% for both genders (45% for girls).

For more than a century, education has used technology to expand beyond the physical limits of schools and university campuses and reach more and nontraditional groups of students. For instance, in the beginning of the last century, Australia and New Zealand used a system of itinerant teachers to educate children and youth living in sparsely inhabited territories. The teachers maintained contact with their students through postal correspondence.

Radio, television, and computer-related technologies have expanded outreach potential further, and higher education institutions have been at the forefront of this expansion. In 1992, 41% of higher education students in Thailand and 38% in Turkey studied at a distance. The China TV University System (Republic of China) and Anadolu University in Turkey each serves more than 500,000 students per year. The United Kingdom Open University has provided education to more than 2 million individuals since it was established about 30 years ago.

Distance learning institutions generally use a mix of technologies that may include printed material, videos, video-conferencing, CD-ROMs, e-mail, and the Internet. Many of them start with less expensive technologies, such as printed materials, and move to faster and more powerful resources as the need for expansion increases.

Expanding access also means integrating populations that have been traditionally excluded from education for cultural and social reasons. In cultures with strict rules regarding interaction between genders, girls may be forced to leave school before puberty to avoid contact with male colleagues and teachers. For girls who remain in school, the rules regarding with whom they may or may not talk make it difficult to succeed. If a girl is having academic difficulties, she may rather fail than address the male teacher.

Technology can promote alternatives for educating women that are more cost-effective than all-female schools without disrupting cultural traditions. Television and radio broadcasts or Internet-based technologies enable girls to continue their studies from home or small learning centers. Technology functions as a neutral mediator, without gender or cultural allegiances, thereby facilitating communication. An essay exercise in a co-educational class at the African Nazarene University that required the use of computers illustrates the potential of ICTs to overcome barriers in communication. Faced with the challenge of learning a new technology, the students forgot tribal rivalries and gender differences to exchange information and work side by side.

For persons with disabilities—who represent another significant and forgotten sector of the world population-technologies provide essential supports enabling them to participate in the educational system and the job market. VisualTek is a camera and monitor that enlarge print materials for people with visual disabilities. Voice synthesizers enable individuals with muscular dystrophies to communicate. Special computer software can be used to ameliorate learning disabilities or to enhance the memory of individuals with traumatic brain injury. Keyboard adaptations enable individuals with motor disabilities to write, and the Internet can connect homebound individuals to classrooms and workplaces.

Lifelong learning and economic development for populations living outside mainstream cultures are two other venues for using ICTs. A multilingual database catalogue offers the artisans' work to a worldwide customer base. The network receives and fills orders and is responsible for quality control.

The internal efficiency of an educational system is measured by its ability to deliver quality education in cost-effective ways. The traditional model for providing primary through tertiary education, adopted across the world, relies on three basic principles.

— Learners must congregate in a building where the teaching/learning process takes place.

— There must be a predetermined path, divided into grades, that leads to a diploma, and students must follow this path, regardless of their interests, needs, or abilities.

— There must be a hierarchic structure where the instructor is the provider of knowledge and the students are the recipients.

The traditional school is, therefore, a physical entity organized into classrooms where learners congregate according to a grade structure and constrained by the limits of space and time. If a school serves students from grades 1 through 12, it must have at least 12 classrooms to accommodate each grade separately. Each classroom must have one teacher. A certain number of teachers require a principal and, often, administrative and teaching support. If the number of students or grades increases, so must the number of needed classrooms, teachers, and support personnel.

Generally, beginning in the seventh grade, another dimension is added to the classroom/grade framework: specialization. From then on, the number of teachers is related to both the number of classrooms and the number of specialties offered. Each school must have at least one mathematics teacher, a science teacher, a social studies teacher, and so on. As the educational level advances, classroom organizations will rely more on specialization than grades, but the framework is maintained. To be cost-effective within this structure, the learning place must have a critical number of students that justifies school construction and maintenance, particularly personnel costs. In areas of low population density, building and maintaining schools to serve the traditional paradigm is economically prohibitive.

The requirement of one specialist per specialty makes secondary schools an even more expensive venture. Some countries sidestep the problem by leaving the solution to individual families, with catastrophic results. If the families choose to move to urban areas and ensure their children's education, they jeopardize their country's fragile economic balance and further deplete the economy of their native regions. If they decide to remain, they jeopardize their children's future. Areas of high population density but weak economy are not free of problems. In this case, the traditional model encourages administrators to accommodate as many students as possible in one classroom to control personnel costs, which leads to overcrowded and unsafe environments that are unfit for learning.

The capacity of ICTs to reach students in any place and at any time has the potential to promote revolutionary changes in the traditional educational paradigm. First, it eliminates the premise that learning time equals classroom time. To avoid overcrowded classrooms, a school may adopt a dual-shift system without reducing its students' actual study time. Students may attend school for half a day and spend the other half involved in educational activities at home, in a library, at work, or in another unconventional setting. They may be required to watch an educational radio/television program and complete related activities, or work on a computer-assisted lesson at the school technology lab or in a community learning center. For areas with low population density, multigrade schools become viable alternatives. While more advanced students listen to an educational program on the radio or watch a television broadcast, the teacher can attend to the students who are in less advanced levels or vice versa.

Traditional educational systems also tend to rely on curricula that were developed at the beginning of the Industrial Revolution and are now disconnected from the realities of the job market. For bright students, these systems offer little in the way of motivation. Eventually, a few extraordinary students will be able to skip a grade, but rushing through the system is not encouraged, and early graduates may find obstacles when they attempt to gain access to the next level. For low-income students, who have less academic support, the schools offer even less: the wealthier schools lure the best teachers, leaving the least prepared for schools in poor and remote areas. When the need to work conflicts with schools' requirements, the student sees no reason to stay in school.

As a result, these systems perpetuate social inequalities, lose many excellent students to boredom, increase the costs of education through high dropout rates and grade retention, and pass on to employers or other systems the costs of retraining their graduates. ICTs have the potential to bring the products of the best teachers to classrooms anywhere in the world. For self-motivated, disciplined students, ICTs can speed the path toward a degree and expand their learning options through self-study. Students can 'shop' courses on the Internet and choose their own program of study and schedules. Students in virtual schools can take extra online courses to graduate earlier or fulfill specific interests and curiosity. For those who need to balance studies with work and family obligations-full- or part-time workers, parents of small children, homebound individuals-this flexibility may be most cost-effective for them.

The management of distance learning is not without difficulty, and, in many cases, local regulations function as obstacles to innovations. However, the demand for more and specialized education is encouraging new arrangements that rely on ICTs to establish communication networks among partner institutions and facilitate student-centered, rather than program-centered organizations, such as the University of the Highlands and Islands.

## Quality of Learning

Research on brain physiology and cognitive psychology is challenging the traditional model of learning as mastery of facts and concepts. The acquisition of knowledge encompasses more than cognition. Perception, for instance, includes at least two basic components:

— an 'objective' component mediated through the senses, which provide the brain with information about the objects surrounding us, their descriptions and location, and our position in relation to them; and

— a 'subjective' component that analyzes the perceived objects through the lens of personal experiences and idiosyncrasies, previous knowledge, and cultural biases.

Images are key components of the process of acquiring and using information because of their ability to condense large amounts of data. Research on working memory proposes that information is stored as images in visuospatial sketch-pads to be used later. The process involves both imageries—the mental reconstructions of objects no longer present to our senses, and imagination—the mental construction of unknown objects. In addition to their role in retention and recall, images have the ability to decode unfamiliar symbols into known representations, a helpful function in language acquisition. Textbook images traditionally have been used in foreign language classes with this decoding function. Images are equally important in the acquisition of science and mathematics, which, similar to a foreign language, have their own symbols, terminologies, and grammatical structures.

Although definitions of quality learning may disagree on details, it is generally accepted that, for learning to occur, the learners must be motivated, basic concepts must be understood, and knowledge must be advanced through more complex, higher-order thinking skill tasks. As move away from linear learning, get closer to how the brain functions. ICTs diversify the systems of representation through the use of various types of stimuli (images, sound, and movement) and address the needs of diverse types of learning. In addition, ICTs have the potential to enhance educational quality by increasing motivation, facilitating acquisition of basic skills, promoting inquiry and exploration, and preparing individuals for the technology-driven world.

An effective teaching/learning process must stimulate intellectual curiosity and offer a sense of enjoyment that will move the students from the passive role of recipients of information to the active role of builders of knowledge. Yet, engaging the learner in this process can be the most challenging task for teachers. ICTs are effective instructional aides to engage students in the learning process. Videos, television, and computer multimedia software provide information that can be authentic and challenging in addition to stimulating students' sensorial apparatus through images, color, sound, and movement.

A training program for bank clerks in the United States was unable to offer on-the-job training because banks refused to accept trainees without some experience. The instructors decided to use videos of actual clerks working at a local bank and trainees role-playing clerk-customer situations. Trainees watched the movies and discussed the tasks involved, potential problems, preferred solutions, and their weaknesses/ strengths. After the videos were introduced, the program placement rates increased from 70% to 93% over a two-year period.

Although radio programs do not have the visual appeal of television or computer, Interactive Radio Instruction (IRI) uses songs, drama-like plots, and comic situations to attract and maintain the attention of students of all ages in rural and low-income areas of developing countries.

Transmission of accumulated knowledge to new generations is an essential component of the educational process. This includes basic skills and information that are at the foundation of more complex knowledge. It would be inefficient to use a time-consuming process, such as inquiry and exploration, to transmit basic information. In addition, nonstructured learning environments based solely on inquiry and exploration may be confusing and overwhelming for some children and youth. These students will do better in well-structured classrooms, where the information is broken into less complex units, thus making it easier to understand. Exposition and practice strategies help to structure the classroom, enhance retention and recall, and cut learning time.

Computers have three attributes that make them powerful aides for drill and practice strategies: large memory, speed, and the capacity to repeat the same task an infinite number of times without reducing performance. In addition, they provide students with the opportunity to learn on their own time and at their own pace.

Computer-aided instruction (CAI) has been used successfully in different settings for basic skill instruction. CAI programs are divided into modules that maintain a hierarchy of concepts and skills. The students have to master each module before being allowed to move to the next, more complex level. An evaluation at the end of each module gives the students immediate feedback. If they respond correctly to a determined percentage of questions, they advance. Otherwise, they repeat the module or enter remedial units until the skills or concepts are mastered. The programme can keep a history of the students' performance-lessons learned, topics with which the student had more difficulty, strategies that improved learning, and how many times the student had to repeat the module. With this information, the teacher can develop an individualised plan that addresses each student's specific weaknesses and strengths. CAI was introduced as an aid in mathematics classes, but it is now used for different disciplines, grade levels, and objectives.

The military has used CAI in training for a long time. Overall, research shows that when CAI is applied well, users learn faster, retain more, and tend to have a more positive attitude toward learning than students receiving traditional instruction. Computers also can be used as auxiliary tools in mathematics and science classes to free teachers' and students' time. While computers work on repetitive tasks, teachers and students can concentrate on analytical activities that require higher-order thinking skills. Elementary and secondary school students who use calculators have higher test scores and better attitudes toward mathematics than their peers who do not use calculators. Elementary school children who use computers and calculators in the classroom were found to understand mathematical concepts much earlier than expected.

Although basic skills and information are essential components of the teaching/learning process, learning is more than information transfer. Learning requires the ability to analyze and synthesize information, use it in diverse circumstances, and propose new lines of inquiry that foster knowledge. Inquiry and exploration are essential strategies to attain those abilities.

ICTs have the potential to restore curiosity to education. ICTs can take students on exciting journeys through time and space. Movies, videos, audio technology, and computer animations bring sound and movement to static textbook lessons and enliven children's reading classes. They also provide social studies and foreign language students with vicarious experiences of distant societies and bygone times. Spreadsheets can store and analyze large amounts of data necessary for complex math and science studies. Computer simulations transform risky and expensive experiments into safe and cost-effective procedures. The Internet offers virtual reality settings where students can manipulate parameters, contexts, and scenarios.

Computer simulations are a good example of the power of technology to improve the learning process. The flight simulator has been used for decades as the initial step in training airplane pilots. A flight simulator offers trainees the opportunity to practice the proper skills to control the plane and deal with emergency situations without risking lives or property loss. Although flight simulators can be complex and expensive machines, no pilot training program would question their utility. Simulators also are becoming essential tools in medical training. Through their use, medical students and residents are introduced to risky and invasive procedures without endangering patients' lives or exposing them to unnecessary pain and discomfort. Simulations are particularly helpful in situations that are too risky, expensive, or time-consuming to allow real-life experiments. For instance, welding simulators have proved to be a cost-effective method to train future welders. Without simulators, this training requires long hours of practice and burning expensive electrodes.

Simulations also enable students to test explosive materials virtually without running the risk of real explosions, and to 'experiment' on animals without the ethical implications of real-life procedures. For elementary and secondary school students-and sometimes even for adults-exploring the Internet can be a fun and enriching experience, or a frustrating adventure in trivia. Teachers and instructors play an important role as guides and facilitators by providing background material and guidelines for the search. They also need to monitor the process, particularly for younger students, who tend to browse the Web, rather than follow structured search plans. Teachers and instructors also are instrumental in helping students to separate unreliable sources from reliable ones and make sense of the large amount of information that may overwhelm them.

Globalization, creativity, and collaboration are key words in the modern workplace, where employers and employees are expected to share knowledge and work together toward common goals. In traditional classrooms, students work in isolation, doing tasks that emphasize conformism and boost competition. Trained in such environments, students may leave the school ill prepared to share ideas, divide tasks, or accept different points of view.

Since ICTs can overcome physical and geographical barriers and facilitate communication, they have the potential to eliminate the artificial boundaries between schools and the outside world, and promote an environment that emphasizes collaboration rather than competition. Videos and computer animations enable students to 'witness' a volcano eruption to learn about pressure, rock formation, or psychological and sociological responses to crises. A simple radio or tape recorder can allow students in a foreign language class to listen to native speech regardless of their teachers' origin. Better yet, with interactive technologies, such as two-way radios or videoconferencing, students can communicate with native speakers without leaving their classrooms.

Videos, DVDs, computer software, and the Internet bring to schools anywhere in the world information that can be obtained only through the use of powerful scientific instruments that no single school can afford. More than any other technology, the Internet opens new opportunities for collaborative work. The Internet has the potential to connect classrooms to research centers and students to actual scientists, as does the Global Learning and Observations to Benefit the Environment (GLOBE). Research on the Apple Classrooms of Tomorrow (ACOT) indicates that technology—rich classrooms promote teamwork and encourage tolerance for alternative viewpoints, two essential skills for increasingly complex and diverse workplaces.

Learning is only one component of the educational process, and quality learning cannot be attained without good teaching. Yet, teachers in general, and good teachers in particular, are in short supply even in developed countries. In the United States, for instance, the National Commission on Teaching and America's Future anticipates the need to hire an additional 2 million teachers in all teaching fields over the next decade to replace an increasingly aging work-force.

For developing countries, in rural areas and in some specialties such as math and science, the teacher shortage has become critical. Simply hiring a teacher does not ensure quality education. To be effective, teachers must keep abreast of new perspectives on learning theories and their area of specialization, a task that becomes impossible when teachers work in distant, isolated areas. The mentoring process that has been used traditionally to prepare new cadres is an extra burden on experienced teachers, particularly in places where they are already in short supply. Some schools of education are using videotaped sessions to prepare new teachers to enter the classroom without relying solely on mentors. The process frequently involves videotaping experienced teachers during regular classroom time. Student teachers observe their experienced peers in action, analyzing in detail the strategies used to present the material and interact with the students.

The trainees then practice mock lessons with a group of peers or volunteer students while being videotaped. Peers and instructors review the tapes, highlighting weaknesses and strengths and making suggestions for improvement. Only after completing this process is the student teacher sent into actual classrooms. Videos can also be used to analyze teaching styles and idiosyncrasies and help educational systems to change their approaches. The Third International Mathematics and Science Study (TIMSS) videotaped mathematics and science teachers in Japan, Germany, and the United States. The study analyzed variations in teaching style and lesson content among the three countries, looking for correlations between those dimensions and students' performance.

ICTs can be used as tools for training and support of teachers, regardless of their geographical dispersion. Scripted lessons in conjunction with educational programs via radio and television, such as the IRI and Telesecundaria programmes, ensure that all students receive quality, updated information, while imparting to inexperienced and generalist teachers the appropriate content knowledge and new pedagogical strategies. The use of technology for teacher training has at least three major advantages: it reduces travel costs, avoids disrupting classroom routines, and familiarizes the teachers with the technology.

The Internet has myriad Websites to help teachers develop or improve lesson plans, exchange ideas, obtain information, and find free animations and simulations to enliven their lessons. Most Internet-based collaborative learning programmes include teacher support and training, and conference proceedings are published regularly on the Web. Chat rooms or forums may become a laboratory for new ideas. For instance, teachers in Soweto, South Africa, used their online connection with schools in Birmingham, U.K., to create a support network and promote discussions on curriculum reform and school management practices. Indeed, contrary to the notion that technology is replacing the teacher, ICTs have expanded the quantity and quality of resources available to making teaching a less lonely endeavour.

## Empowerment of Teacher Education

More important still, research indicates that the introduction of ICTs for educational purposes has the potential to bring positive changes to teaching practices. Around 2,000 teachers and school principals across the United States, the teachers stated that the technology helped them to become more effective (92% of respondents) and creative (88%). Both teachers and administrators agreed that technology had reinforced instruction, and functioned as a motivator for the students, who were more prone to ask questions and participate in the lessons.

Despite this potential for training and support, ICTs have not been accepted easily among teachers. Some complain that scripted lessons take away their ability to address students' individual differences and improve their own teaching strategies. Others fear that technologies will reduce the role of teachers in defining curriculum and educational strategies, or totally replace them.

Education policy development is an intricate process that requires reliable, timely, user-friendly data. ICTs can be valuable for storing and analyzing data on education indicators; student assessments; educational, physical, and human infrastructure; and cost and finance. The use of computer-related technology is particularly helpful in this field. For instance, administrators and policy makers can construct virtual scenarios around different policy options to determine needs and analyze potential consequences. Each scenario can be analyzed and evaluated systematically, not only in terms of its educational desirability, but also in terms of financial affordability, feasibility, and sustainability over a sufficient period of time to show results.

The same elements of computing and telecommunications equipment and service that have made businesses more efficient and cost-effective can be applied to schools and educational systems. ICTs can help administrators and school principals to streamline operations, monitor performance, and improve use of physical and human resources. More than other technologies, computer-related technologies have the potential to support the management of complex, standards-related instructional processes in relatively simple ways. They also can promote communication among schools, parents, central decision makers, and businesses, thus fostering accountability, public support, and connectivity with the marketplace.

The effectiveness of ICTs-the realization of their potential-depends to a large extent on the context and quality of application. Moreover, since ICTs are only tools for education, it is difficult to isolate the factors that may be contributing to a positive result-such as educational philosophy, quality of teaching, parent support, and students' characteristics. With these caveats in mind, evidence from large studies and meta-analyses suggests that use of ICTs, particularly computer technologies, is correlated to positive academic outcomes, including higher test scores, better attitudes toward schools, and better understanding of abstract concepts.

A longitudinal study of a statewide experiment with computers in the classroom found that those most in need of help-low-income, low-achieving students, and students with disabilities-made the most gains. In addition to better performance in traditional measures of academic achievement, a secondary benefit of ICTs in education is to familiarize new generations with the technologies that have become integral components of the modern world. However, research on the effect of ICTs on academic achievement continues to be open to criticism. Critics deny positive findings as the result of flawed studies, while supporters promote positive results without sufficiently evaluating the quality of the studies. In the final analysis, ICTs are as good as how they are used. The path from potential to effectiveness is neither easy nor automated.

ICTs for education in the context of the educational enterprise's struggle to be relevant, responsive, and effective in meeting the challenges of the 21st century, by providing the whole spectrum of education services to everyone, anywhere, anytime with a focus on learning acquisition and teacher empowerment—all under conditions of an ever-expanding base of education clientele and limited physical and human resources.

Technologies are only tools-but powerful ones. They have the potential to contribute to different facets of educational development and effective learning: expanding access, promoting efficiency, improving the quality of learning, enhancing the quality of teaching, vitalizing management systems, boosting the possibilities for lifelong learning, and offering e-training for the workplace. But there is a distinction between potential and effectiveness. For the potential of ICTs to be realized, constraints have to be alleviated, and a set of co and prerequisites must be met. The parameters for success cover a wide spectrum, including education policies and strategies; physical, hardware, and software infrastructures; human and financial resources; and implementation modalities.

Many countries struggling with providing minimal levels of educational services to their populations are questioning the suitability of ICTs for them. Unfortunately, no country or institution has the luxury to think in an orderly and sequential fashion about providing educational opportunities in terms of levels of education, domains of access, degrees of quality, or ICT modalities. It is always a question of striking a balance between different demands. ICTs are experimented with, introduced, and integrated into many educational systems and institutions worldwide, through educational radio and television programs, open universities, virtual high schools, exciting children's software, computer-enhanced programs, and Web-based learning opportunities. The private sector has entered the field vigorously, with corporate universities, e-training programs, and educational offerings on the Internet. But many of these efforts are on the margin. Most countries are still far from reengineering their educational systems to make the best use of ICTs, and the objective of effective learning for everyone, anytime, anywhere is far from being fulfilled.

The challenges facing education worldwide will escalate, and the struggle between needs and resources will deepen. The quest for radical solutions will intensify, and the pressure to 'do something' with ICTs will keep mounting.

Experience has shown that effective integration of ICTs into education and learning systems is not instantaneous; it takes sustained hard and deliberate effort, keeping in mind three considerations:

— ICTs for education, like any educational activity or reform, require a long gestation period. Therefore, commitments, efforts, investments, and implementation schemes must be sustained over a long period of time. For instance, let us keep in mind that experimenting with Web-based learning for far less time than it takes one cohort of students to go through school.

— Integration of ICTs into education is a radical innovation and should be treated as such. Innovations require building a solid base of knowledge and commitment, interacting with interest groups, generating and testing different options, experimentation, planning for large-scale implementation, critical mass application, and a mind open to modification and adjustment. It is obvious that an incremental issue-specific approach is always superior to a comprehensive strategic approach . . . . A step-by-step approach allows experimentation and adjustment and does not have high political and institutional demands. On the other hand, this approach may lead to "low-risk" quick-fixes, and inadequate investment in terms of political capital and other resources to carry the reform off successfully. The success stories of . . . case studies have shown that to solve sector-wide problems in the context of political and economic demands, it is prudent to start with a limited incremental phase, but this should be succeeded in time by a comprehensive strategic approach. The timing and speed of this evolution should be gauged to the degree of acceptability of the reform by the stakeholders, and the implementation capacity of the system.

— Educators (teachers and education administrators at all levels) are central to ensuring that ICTs will be introduced and integrated properly into the teaching/ learning process. One should not assume that educators will be supportive naturally. ICTs transform dynamics of the education enterprise; they change the roles of teachers, administrators, students, and parents. At the same time, ICTs can break school insulation; they connect schools to a world beyond the immediate environment and make them more transparent to parents and communities at large. Educators need to be convinced of the benefits of ICTs for them and their professions and must be brought actively into the early stages of planning and development.

Effective application of ICTs requires creativity in exploiting the technologies of today and imagining the potential of the technologies of tomorrow. Current technologies have not been well explored and exploited. Compared to business, commerce, and entertainment, education is very far behind.

There is a whole world out there of animations, simulations, digital pads, electronic books, virtual presentations via Webcasting, chat rooms, videoconferencing, machine translation, speech technology, handheld computers, electronic white boards, and virtual reality. Combining these technologies provides learning environments beyond imagination, but within our reach. But strategies for using ICTs for education solutions should not be driven by the potential of current technologies alone.

The world of ICTs is exploding with new inventions, and the lifetime of many technologies is shorter than the lifetime of educational reform. Yet, it is hard to imagine what technologies will exist in 10 years. Only 15 years ago, the hottest items were fax machines, a slow computer, and a dot matrix printer. There were no e-mail, Web sites, digital radio, or application CDs. Technology is moving faster than our imaginations; however, education strategists need to keep their fingers on the pulse of technological innovation. Four areas are of particular interest to educators:

— sensors connected to computers that can sense speech, physical conditions, and even brain waves;

— Internet 2, with enormous capacity and speed

— wearable PCs that will change the whole notion of computer infrastructure, networking, and configuration; and

— nanotechnology (a nanometer is one billionth of a meter), which may lead to such small computers that, by 2020, may be able to use the Internet to download not just software, but hardware as well.

ICTs for education call for dramatic changes in education systems, heavy investment, and long-term commitments; yet, the knowledge base to make decisions and choices is not commensurate with the enormity of what is required. Meanwhile, educational technologies are about education and learning. While our knowledge of learning has improved significantly as a result of advancements in cognitive and brain science, research into the effect of ICT interventions on the learning process, including neuro-physiology, is nearly nonexistent.

A significant body of research on ICTs' effectiveness is available, but it is often contradictory, difficult to interpret, and even more difficult to use in the policy-making process. What is needed is more large-scale longitudinal research, policy-related studies, comparative analyses across countries and contexts, cost-effectiveness measurements and piloting. Despite its shortcomings, current knowledge tends to accumulate in the hands of a few, more often than not driven by powerful economic interests and concentrated in the hands of a few institutions (private and public). Such knowledge, to a large extent, is concentrated in economically and technologically advanced countries, and sometimes in institutions that are not traditionally part of the educational or academic community.

Local, regional, and international mechanisms must be created to build a solid knowledge base of ideas, issues, research results, case studies, best practices, and resources. Such knowledge clearinghouses will offer up-to-date information and syntheses to assist decision makers and practitioners in the design and implementation of educational technology programs without reinventing the wheel or repeating others' mistakes. They also will help in identifying knowledge gaps and topics for research.

Unfortunately, however, research, broad evaluation, and development have not attracted much funding. Countries and institutions seem to be willing to invest huge amounts of money in ICT programmes with little knowledge of their potential benefits, but are unwilling to invest a small fraction of these amounts in research and development to protect their large investments and improve their effectiveness. A knowledge base totally derived from market supply will have many gaps, which will decrease its usefulness. Also, current conditions create distortions in the knowledge 'market.' For instance, some current players may have no incentive to invest in sophisticated studies. As gaps are identified and distortions in knowledge generation detected, public resources need to be invested to fill these gaps and redress these distortions.

As more educational software and entire courses of study become available via radio, TV, the Internet, or some combination of these, whether free or fee-based, the issue of quality assurance becomes acute. Regional and international cooperation is needed to establish standards, guidelines, and accreditation mechanisms. It is in the interest of all partners, including those in the economic sector, to introduce coherence and transparency into this new, mushrooming market.

## Components of ICTs in Teacher Education

Teacher education unit, state, region or country adopts or

adapts a set of standards for determining how technology will be infused throughout their programmes, it is critical that faculty in the teacher education programmes be included in the planning effort.

The faculty will plan for ICTs in teacher development considering their own conditions, culture, and context. During this collaborative planning phase, the teacher education unit and other university units providing courses for pre-service teachers (i.e. teacher candidates) should develop plans that not only address the four key components within the framework, but also the elements that support long-term implementation of the key components-leadership and vision, context and culture, planning and management of change, and lifelong learning. These elements are necessary for a supportive environment and a successful, self-sustaining implementation of technology infusion within the teacher education programme.

As educational entities have implemented ICTs in teacher education, researchers and evaluators have identified barriers that prevent or restrict successful technology infusion. In US, ISTE has compiled a list of the most commonly cited conditions necessary to create learning environments conducive to powerful uses of technology.

When planning for implementation of ICTs in teacher education, the planning team should consider each essential condition and note whether, and to what extent, it is present. The context, culture, and extent of collaboration among stakeholders will affect how adequately the conditions are met and determine what types of strategies might solicit support if the essential conditions are not currently present.

From the administration to the grounds personnel, there is an understanding of, commitment to, and sense of advocacy for the implementation of technology. When the implementation of a technology initiative is problematic, a major reason often cited is a breakdown in the common understanding of the institution's goals among those who hold the decision-making power. These situations can occur over something as simple as unlocking the door to a lab, or as complex as modifying existing operational budgets to provide allocations for technology funding.

Facilitating the integration of technology may require a change in policy or rules, and the decision-makers have to be willing to look at the situation, forge compromises when necessary, and ensure communication among all parties. The collaborative environment necessary for creating a shared vision is also needed to sustain that vision.

The fact that educators need access to current technologies, software, and telecommunications networks seems simple. However, this access must be consistent across all the environments that are part of the preparation of teachers.

*Table 1. Essential Conditions for Implementing ICTs in Teacher Education*

| | |
|---|---|
| **Shared Vision** | There is proactive leadership and administrative support from the entire system. |
| **Access** | Educators have access to current technologies, software, and telecommunications networks. |
| **Skilled Educators** | Educators are skilled in the use of technology for learning. |
| **Professional Development** | Educators have consistent access to professional development in |

| | |
|---|---|
| | support of technology use in teaching and learning. |
| **Technical Assistance** | Educators have technical assistance for maintaining and using the technology. |
| Content Standards and Curriculum Resources | Educators are knowledgeable in their subject matter and current in the content standards and teaching methodologies in their discipline. |
| **Student-Centred Teaching** | Teaching in all settings encompasses student-centred approaches to learning. |
| **Assessment** | There is continuous assessment of the effectiveness of technology for learning. |
| **Community Support** | The community and school partners provide expertise, support, and resources. |
| **Support Policies** | School and university policies, financing, and rewards structures are in place to support technology in learning. (ISTE, 2000) |

Most teacher education programmes involve several entities, including at least a college or university and one or more schools in the P-12 range. The access to funding and other resources may vary greatly among these partners, yet ideally, access should be adequate and consistent throughout the educational experience of students in the process of becoming teachers.

Creative partnerships are often required to make this happen. Additionally, there needs to be access to technology appropriate to the subject areas being studied, such as word processing programs and Internet access in English, or computer labs and microscopes for science labs.

The technology should be accessible immediately when it is the best route to the information or tools needed by pre-service teachers, teachers, and students. Furthermore, university model classrooms are important for determining the way technology should be used in the P-12 environment. There should be an instructor station with a presentation system and 4-6 stations for pre-serv-ice teachers.

The teacher candidates need to see and experience models that demonstrate the kind of access desired in the classroom. In addition to ICT access in their coursework, pre-service teachers must have technology access in their student teaching environments and in their classrooms in the induction year and beyond.

Otherwise, opportunities to use technology tools for teaching students or communication tools for mentoring or staying connected with parents will be limited. The educators who work with teacher candidates must be skilled in the use of technology for learning. They must be able to apply technology in the presentation and administration of their coursework and facilitate the appropriate use of technology by their teacher candidates.

Ongoing opportunities for professional development should be available to university and P-12 faculty and administrators who participate in the preparation of teachers. The venues and delivery mechanisms should take into consideration issues of time, location, distance, credit options, and so on. Professional development is not a one-time event it should be focused on the needs of the faculty member, teacher, or administrator and sustained through coaching and periodic updates.

Educators need technical assistance to use and maintain technology. The focus of the faculty member, teacher, and pre-service teacher should be on teaching and learning, not on maintaining and repairing the technology beyond basic troubleshooting procedures. When the technology does not function well, a learning opportunity is lost and faculty frustration grows.

Timely technical assistance is imperative for faculty and candidates to feel confident that they can use technology in their teaching and learning. There are many ways technical assistance can be obtained, including asking community members or student assistants to maintain a help desk. It is a critical factor for success in implementing ICTs. Educators must be knowledgeable in the content, standards, and teaching methodologies of their disciplines. Teacher candidates must learn to use technology in powerful, meaningful ways in the context of teaching content.

Technology brings relevant resources from the real world to subject area content, provides tools for analysing and synthesizing data, and conveys content through a variety of media and formats. Pre-service teachers should learn to use technology in ways that meet the content standards and the technology standards for students and teachers.

Teaching in all settings should encompass student-centred approaches to learning. Technology should not be used only as a tool for demonstration, as an electronic overhead projector or blackboard; rather the use of technology by students should be an integral part of instruction.

In student-centred approaches to learning, students become the source for problems investigated. Students and teacher candidates must have opportunities to identify problems, collect and analyze data, draw conclusions, and convey results using electronic tools to accomplish these tasks. Faculty should model the use of ICTs to demonstrate their usefulness and appropriateness for collaboration, acquisition of resources, analysis and synthesis, presentation, and publication.

In addition to assessing teaching and student outcomes, institutions should continuously assess the effectiveness of technology for learning throughout the entire teacher preparation environment. The data obtained from this continuous assessment will:

— inform the learning strategies used,

— ensure that the vision for technology-use maintains the appropriate direction,

— pinpoint potential problems, and

— provide data for altering policies and instructional strategies or for acquiring resources.

Changes made over time due to technology innovation will exemplify informed decision-making. The visioning process includes the community and school partners who provide expertise, support, and resources for technology implementation. The community must see that technology is a valuable tool for prospective teachers and their students, and must be willing to support it in the political process from the boardroom to the state house.

Policies can either support or hinder the implementation of technology. As decision-makers develop new policies, they must consider how the policies affect acquisition of and access to technology. Some major barriers to the use of technology relate to faculty expectations about incentives and reward structures. The expectation for the use of technology must cut across all subject areas and teacher preparation contexts so that faculty and teacher candidates are assured that their work will be valued.

Policies related to technical assistance should also support the use of technology rather than obstruct it. For example, although firewalls are essential in the university environment, there are ways to provide dial-up and remote access while maintaining the security of campus servers. Likewise, at the school level, there are ways to control students ' Internet access to unwanted images and information while maintaining an environment of exploration and inquiry.

Teachers and teacher educators cannot be expected to implement what they have learned about effective use of ICTs without the presence of essential conditions in their work environment.

In planning the integration of ICTs into teacher education, it is important for teacher education institutions to understand the knowledge and skills necessary for teachers to effectively use ICTs in their instruction. They must also understand the institution's level of readiness to integrate technology into the teacher education curriculum. To accomplish these goals requires that the teacher education institution understand the benchmarks, standards, and guidelines for ICTs in teacher education. It is also important that they have access to tools that help them assess their level of readiness and progress in infusing ICTs into the teacher education programmes.

# 2

# Framework for ICTs in Education

Teacher education institutions may either assume a leadership role in the transformation of education or be left behind in the swirl of rapid technological change. For education to reap the full benefits of ICTs in learning, it is essential that pre-service and in-service teachers have basic ICT skills and competencies.

Teacher education institutions and programmes must provide the leadership for pre-service and in-service teachers and model the new pedagogies and tools for learning. They must also provide leadership in determining how the new technologies can best be used in the context of the culture, needs, and economic conditions within their country.

Teacher education institutions also need to develop strategies and plans to enhance the teaching-learning process within teacher education programmes and to assure that all future teachers are well prepared to use the new tools for learning. As noted in the UNESCO

World Education Report, Teachers and Teaching in a Changing World, the young generation is entering a world that is changing in all spheres: scientific and technological, political, economic, social, and cultural.

The emergence of the 'knowledge-based ' society is changing the global economy and the status of education. There is growing awareness among policy-makers, business leaders and educators that the educational system designed to prepare learners for an agrarian or industrially-based economy will not provide students with the knowledge and skills they will need to thrive in the 21st century's knowledge-based economy and society.

The new knowledge-based global society is one in which:

— the world's knowledge base doubles every 2 -3 years;

— 7,000 scientific and technical articles are published each day;

— data sent from satellites orbiting the earth transmit enough data to fill 19 million volumes every two weeks;

These new possibilities exist largely as the result of two converging forces. First the quantity of information available in the world-much of it relevant to survival and basic well-being-is exponentially greater than that available only a few years ago, and the rate of its growth is accelerating.

A synergistic effect occurs when important information is coupled with a second modern advance-the new capacity to communicate among people of the world. The opportunity exists to harness this force and use it positively, consciously, and with design, in order to contribute to meeting defined learning needs. As is the case for other sectors of the wider economy and society, education will need to come to terms with the new technologies.

This could require substantial public and private sector investments in software research and development, purchase of hardware, and refurbishment of schools, It will be difficult for national policy-makers to resist finding the necessary resources, whatever their sensibilities for expenditure on education, although without international co-operation and assistance the poorest countries could fall still further behind.

The challenge confronting our educational systems is how to transform the curriculum and teaching-learning process to provide students with the skills to function effectively in this dynamic, information-rich, and continuously changing environment.

The technology-based global economy also poses challenges to countries as national economies become more internationalized, with the increasing flow of information, technology, products, capital, and people between nations. This new economic environment is creating a new era of global competition for goods, services, and expertise.

All of these changes are producing dramatic shifts in the political, economic and social structures of many countries around the world. In industrialized nations, the economic base is shifting from industry to information. This shift also demands new knowledge and skills in the work force.

ICTs have changed the nature of work and the types of skills needed in most fields and professions. While they have, on the one hand, created a wide array of new jobs, many of which did not even exist ten years ago, they have also replaced the need for many types of unskilled or low-skilled workers.

For example, the new 'smart agricultural equipment, using advance digital and industrial technology, is able to do the work previously done with a large number of low-skilled agricultural workers. In addition, new manufacturing plants are requiring fewer low-skilled workers.

A Canadian study notes, for example, that in high-tech companies only 10% of the work force is comprised of unskilled workers. These trends pose new challenges to educational systems to prepare students with the knowledge and skills needed to thrive in a new and dynamic environment of continuous technological change and accelerating growth in knowledge production.

Education is at the confluence of powerful and rapidly shifting educational, technological and political forces that will shape the structure of educational systems across the globe for the remainder of this century.

Many countries are engaged in a number of efforts to effect changes in the teaching/learning process to prepare students for an information and technology-based society. The UNESCO World Education Report notes that the new technologies challenge traditional conceptions of both teaching and learning and, by reconfiguring how teachers and learners gain access to knowledge, have the potential to transform teaching and learning processes.

ICTs provide an array of powerful tools that may help in transforming the present isolated, teacher-centred and text-bound classrooms into rich, stu-dent-focused, interactive knowledge environments. To meet these challenges, schools must embrace the new technologies and appropriate the new ICT tools for learning.

They must also move toward the goal of transforming the traditional paradigm of learning. To accomplish this goal requires both a change in the traditional view of the learning process and an understanding of how the new digital technologies can create new learning environments in which students are engaged learners, able to take greater responsibility for their own learning and constructing their own knowledge.

Thomas Kuhn suggests that revolutions in science come about when the old theories and methods will not solve new problems. He calls these changes in theory and methods a "paradigm shift." There is widespread concern that the educational experiences provided in many schools will not prepare students well for the future.

Many educators and business and government leaders believe that creating a paradigm shift in views of the learning process, coupled with applications of the new information technologies, may play an important role in bringing educational systems into alignment with the knowledge-based, information-rich society.

## Traditional Teacher learning

The teacher is the expert and the dispenser of knowledge to the students. It is largely a 'broadcast ' model of learning where the teacher serves as the repository and transmitter of knowledge to the students. The traditional educational paradigm is often characterized by the following views of learning.

Learning is hard. Many view learning as a difficult and often tedious process. According to this view, if students are having fun or enjoying what they are doing in a learning activity, they probably are not learning.

Learning is based on a deficit model of the student. The system strives to identify deficiencies and weaknesses of the student. Based on noted deficiencies, students are tracked, categorized, remediated or failed. The impact of the deficit model of student learning is most obvious in compensatory education programmes.

As implied by the term, compensatory education is designed to make up or remediate learning that some children, particularly poor minority children, do not have, but which the curriculum and structure of schooling assume are common to all children. Bruer, in his book, Schools for Thought, notes that research overwhelmingly concentrates on the weaknesses of poor children.

Very little research has been done on their strengths. In addition, the weaknesses identified are often deficiencies in terms of the traditional organization and content of schooling. Very little thought has been given to the idea of changing schooling to accommodate new kinds of students; all the effort has gone to changing the students so that they will fit into the schools.

In addition, the underlying assumptions about poor students ' motivation, language, and conceptual development have..." militated against offering them a literacy of thoughtfulness and have favoured a low-level, atomized, concrete, basic-skills curriculum. The language of that curriculum has been so simplified that it is both boring and artificial. It has been stripped of its richness and context and made fundamentally meaningless, which is to say unab-sorbable by normal people, except through memorization, whose effects last only few hours or days."

Learning is a process of information transfer and reception. Learning is an individual/solitary process. In a study of schools in the United States, the National Assessment of Educational Progress noted that most students spend long hours working alone at their desks completing worksheets or repetitive tasks. A London Times survey of English school children indicated that students almost unanimously rejected this daily ordeal of dull and ritualistically solitary classroom activity and called for a broader and more exciting curriculum. The Times reported, however, that there was little evidence of changes in the curriculum that would respond to the students' wishes.

Learning is facilitated by breaking content/ instruction into small isolated units .The educational system is often geared more to categorizing and analyzing patches of knowledge than to sewing them together. In 1993, Bruer notes that the technology of mass education is quite adept at "breaking knowledge and skills into thousands of little standardized, decontextualized pieces, which could be taught and tested one at a time." Neil Postman in his book, Teaching as a Subversive Activity ,states that our educational systems break knowledge and experience into "subjects, relentlessly turning wholes into parts, history into events without restoring continuity."

Learning is a linear process .Frequently, the textbook or teacher provides only one linear path through a narrowly bounded content area or sequence of standardized instructional units. For example, in a mathematics text only one correct problem solution trail may be offered for a specific subclass of problems. However, the problems encountered in daily life (or in mathematics) seldom have only one · solution path or sequence.

## The Process of Learning

In contrast to the traditional teaching-learning paradigm, a new paradigm of the teaching-learning process is emerging, based on three decades of research in human learning, that encompasses the following views of the human learning process:

— *Learning is a natural process:* The natural state of the brain is to learn, however, not everyone learns in the same way. There are different learning, perceptual and personality styles that must be considered in the design of learning experiences for the individual student. Given interesting and rich learning environments, and supportive and stimulating teachers, students will learn. Teachers have often noted that children who appear disruptive or to have short attention spans when confronted with typical classroom instruction, may spend long periods engaged in meaningful and interesting comput-er-related activities.

— *Learning is a social process:* The communal context of knowledge and learning is beginning to be rediscovered, as evidenced by the rapid growth of quality circles and computer-supported collaborative work in business, government, medicine, and higher education. As Vygotsky noted long ago, students learn best in collaboration with peers, teachers, parents, and others when they are actively engaged in meaningful, interesting tasks. ICTs provide opportunities for teachers and students to collaborate with others across the country and across the globe. They also provide new tools to support this collaborative learning in the classroom and online.

— *Learning is an active and not a passive process:* In most fields, people are faced with the challenge of producing knowledge rather than simply reproducing knowledge. To allow students to move toward competence, they must be actively engaged in the learning process, in activities such as solving real problems, producing original writing, completing scientific research projects (rather than simply studying about science), dialoguing with others on important issues, providing artistic and musical performances, and constructing physical objects.

  The traditional curriculum asks students only to recall and describe what others have accomplished or produced. While all production of knowledge must be based on an understanding of prior knowledge, the mere reproduction of knowledge, without its connection to the production of knowledge, is largely a passive activity that neither fully engages nor challenges the student.

— *Learning may either be linear or non-linear:* Much of what now happens in schools appears based on the notion that the mind works like a serial processor that is designed to process only one piece of information at a time in sequential order. But the mind is a wonderful parallel processor that may attend to and process many different types of information simultaneously.

Cognitive theory and research sees learning as a reorganization of knowledge structures. The knowledge structures are stored in semantic memory as schema or cognitive maps. Students "learn" by augmenting, combining, and rearranging a collection of cognitive maps, many of which overlap or are interconnected through a complex network of associations.

There are many ways that students may acquire and process information and assimilate it into their existing knowledge structures. Although some knowledge domains, such as mathematics, may perhaps lend themselves to a linear approach, not all learning can or should occur linearly.

— *Learning is integrative and contextualized:* Pribram's holistic brain theory suggests that information presented globally is more easily assimilated than information presented only in a sequence of information elements. It is also easier for students to see relations and to make connections.

The teacher's role is to help them in several ways to make connections and to integrate knowledge. Learning is based on a strength model of student abilities, interest, and culture. Based on the work of Howard Gardner and others, schools are beginning to consider the specific strengths and interests that students bring to the learning environment, and are designing learning activities that build on student strengths rather than focusing only upon remediating weaknesses.

In addition, schools increasingly recognize diversity as a resource rather than a problem in the classroom. In contrast to the remedial and standardized concept of instruction, diversity and individual differences are valued and the learning process is designed to build on the strengths and assets brought by the learner to the classroom. Learning is assessed through task completion, products, and real problem solving of both individual and group efforts.

Rather than simply evaluating students through paper and pencil tests, assessments are made using portfolios of actual performances and work in both collaborative and individual learning tasks.

The traditional view of the learning process is typically teacher-centred, with teachers doing most of the talking and intellectual work, while students are passive receptacles of the information provided. This is not to indicate that the traditional lecture method is without value, as it allows the teacher to quickly convey lots of information to students and is a useful strategy for recall or rote learning. However, it is not the most effective way to help students develop and use higher order cognitive skills to solve complex realworld problems.

Today's students no longer want to be passive recipients in the information transfer model of learning. Rather they want to be active participants in the learning process. There is growing recognition that today's world requires that students be able to work collaboratively with others, think critically and creatively, and reflect on their own learning processes.

As technology has created change in all aspects of society, it is also changing our expectations of what students must learn in order to function in the new world economy. Students will have to learn to navigate through large amounts of information, to analyse and make decisions, and to master new knowledge domains in an increasingly technological society. They will need to be lifelong learners, collaborating with others in accomplishing complex tasks, and effectively using different systems for representing and communicating knowledge to others.

A shift from teacher-centred instruction to learner-centred instruction is needed to enable students to acquire the new 21st century knowledge and skills. The following table identifies the shift that will take place in changing from a focus on teaching to a focus on learning.

Shifting the emphasis from teaching to learning can create a more interactive and engaging learning environment for teachers and learners. This new environment also involves a change in the roles of both teachers and students. As shown in Table 1, the role of the teacher will change from knowledge transmitter to that of learning facilitator, knowledge guide, knowledge navigator and co-learner with the student.

*Table 1*

| | |
|---|---|
| **Changes in Teacher Role** | |
| A shift from: | A shift to: |
| Knowledge transmitter, primary source of information, content expert, and source of all answers | Learning facilitator, collaborator,coach,mentor, knowledge navigator, and co-learner |
| Teacher controls and directs all aspects of learning | Teacher gives students more options and responsibilities for their own learning |
| **Changes in Student Role** | |
| A shift from: | A shift to: |
| Passive recipient of information | Reproducing knowledge |
| Active participant in the learning process | Producing and sharing knowledge,participating at times as expert |
| Learning as a solitary activity | Learning collaboratively with others |

The new role does not diminish the importance of the teacher but requires new knowledge and skills. Students will have greater responsibility for their own learning in this environment as they seek out, find, synthesize, and share their knowledge with others. ICTs provide powerful tools to support the shift to student-centred learning and the new roles of teachers and students. The new views of the learning process and the shift to student-centred learning have emerged based on cognitive learning research and the confluence of several theories that have informed our understanding of the nature and context of learning.

Some of the most prominent theories include: sociocultural theory, constructivism theory, self-regulated learning, situated cognition, cognitive apprenticeship, problem-based learning, cognitive flexibility theory, and distributed cognition. Each of these theories is based on the same underlying assumptions that learners are active agents, purposefully seeking and constructing knowledge within a meaningful context.

The learner engages in authentic tasks in authentic contexts using authentic tools and is assessed through authentic performance. The environment provides the learner with coaching and scaffolding in developing knowledge and skills. It provides a rich collaborative environment enabling the learner to consider diverse and multiple perspectives to address issues and solve problems. It also provides opportunities for the student to reflect on his or her learning.

Although the new learning environment can be created without the use of technology, it is clear that ICTs can provide powerful tools to help learners access vast knowledge resources, collaborate with others, consult with experts, share knowledge, and solve complex problems using cognitive tools.

ICTs also provide learners with powerful new tools to represent their knowledge with text, images, raphics, and video. The new view of the learning process is based on research that has emerged from theoretical frameworks related to human learning.

Many reflect a constructivism view of the learning process. In this view, learners are active agents who engage in their own knowledge construction by integrating new information into their schema or mental structures. The learning process is seen as a process of "meaning-making" in socially, culturally, historically ,and politically situated contexts.

In a constructivism learning environment, students construct their own knowledge by testing ideas and approaches based on their prior knowledge and experience, applying these to new tasks, contexts and situations, and integrating the new knowledge gained with preexisting intellectual constructs.

A constructivist environment involves developing learning communities comprised of students, teachers and experts who are engaged in authentic tasks in authentic contexts closely related to work done in the real world. A constructivist learning environment also provides opportunities for learners to experience multiple perspectives. The constructivist learning environment also emphasizes authentic assessment of learning rather than the traditional paper/pencil test.

Vygotsky's sociocultural theory of human learning describes learning as a social process and the origination of human intelligence in society or culture. The major theme of Vygotsky's theoretical framework is that social interaction plays a fundamental role in the development of cognition. Vygotsky believed everything is learned on two levels. First, through interaction with others, and then integrated into the individual's mental structure. A second aspect of Vygotsky's theory is the idea that the potential for cognitive development is limited to a "zone of proximal development" (ZPD).

A teacher or more experienced peer is able to provide the learner with "scaffolding" to support the student's evolving understanding of knowledge domains or development of complex skills.

Collaborative learning, discourse, modelling, and scaffolding are strategies for supporting the intellectual knowledge and skills of learners and facilitating intentional learning. The implications of Vygotsky theory are that learners should be provided with socially rich environments in which to explore knowledge domains with their fellow students, teachers and outside experts.

ICTs can be used to support the learning environment by providing tools for discourse, discussions, collaborative writing, and problem-solving, and by providing online support systems to scaffold students ' evolving understanding and cognitive growth.

The goals of problem-based learning (PBL) are to develop higher order thinking skills by providing students with authentic and complex problems and cases. This approach to learning provides a more authentic context for learning and engages students in authentic tasks. It is used frequently in fields such as engineering, medicine and architecture, and has been increasingly applied to K-12 settings.

Through the process of working together, articulating theories, creating hypotheses, and critically discussing the ideas of others, students move to deeper levels of understanding of the problem. The self-directed learning strategies developed in PBL may help foster students ' lifelong learning..

Distributed cognition emphasizes that cognitive growth is fostered through interaction with others and involves dialogue and discourse, making private knowledge public and developing shared understandings.

Tools for online collaboration have been designed to support collaborative knowledge construction and sharing in the classroom. Cognitive Flexibility theory theory asserts that people acquire knowledge in ill-structured domains by constructing multiple representations and linkages among knowledge units. It also notes that learners revisit the same concepts and principles in a variety of contexts.

The theory is useful in understanding how knowledge is transferred in ill-structured knowledge domains. Cognitive apprenticeship is a term for the instructional process in which teachers or more experienced or knowledgeable peers provide 'scaffolds ' to support learners ' cognitive growth and development. Cognitive apprenticeship permits students to learn through their interactions, construct knowledge, and share knowledge-building experiences with the other members of the learning community.

ICTs provide powerful new tools to support cognitive apprenticeships, enabling groups to share online workspaces to collaboratively develop artifacts and intellectual products. They also make possible tele-apprenticeships, in which an expert is able to work with or mentor a student who may be thousands of miles distant.

Situated learning emphasizes the use of apprenticeship, coaching, collaboration, authentic contexts, tasks, activities and cognitive tools. It occurs when students work on authentic tasks that take place in real-world settings. Learning is viewed as a function of the activity, context and culture in which it occurs, which contrasts with most classroom learning which is abstract and out of context.

Situated cognition theory emphasizes providing an authentic context for the learner and encouraging social interaction and collaboration in the learning environment. Through collaborative problem solving, dialogue, and discussion students are able to develop deeper levels of understanding of a problem or knowledge domain.

Self-regulated learners are those who are aware of their own knowledge and understandings, i.e., what they know and what they do not know or need to understand. It combines self-observation, self-judgment, and self-reaction. Self-regulation plays a crucial role in all phases of learning and has the potential to increase the meaningfulness of students ' classroom learning.

ICT tools can be used to make students ' tacit knowledge public and to help them develop metacognitive skills and become more reflective and self-regulated learners. These theories that undergird the new views of the learning process help shape the new pedagogies for learning.

Ultimately, the power of ICTs will be determined by the ability of teachers to use the new tools for learning to create rich, new, and engaging learning environments for their students.

Self-regulated learners are those who are aware of their own knowledge and understandings, i.e., what they know and what they do not know or need to understand. It combines self-observation, self-judgment, and self-reaction. Self-regulation plays a crucial role in all phases of learning and has the potential to increase the meaningfulness of students ' classroom learning. ICT tools can be used to make students ' tacit knowledge public and to help them develop metacognitive skills and become more reflective and self-regulated learners.

## ICTs and Teacher Education

In many of the countries targeted with the ICT curriculum, ICTs are in the early stages of development in commerce, industry, and particularly, in society. Communities and regions may have very limited resources, so it is important to undertake a careful analysis using an ethnographic approach to develop an organic strategy for the growth and development of education and teacher education that takes advantage of ICTs.

The vision is not simply of ICTs, but of better education facilitated through the adoption and promotion of ICTs. The Society for Information Technology and Teacher Education has identified basic principles for development of effective ICT teacher education. These are:

— *Technology should be infused into the entire teacher education programme*: Throughout their teacher education experience, students should learn about and with technology and how to incorporate it into their own teaching. Restricting technology experiences to a single course or to a single area of teacher education, such as methods courses, will not prepare students to be technology-using teachers. Pre-service teacher education students should learn about a wide range of educational technologies across their professional preparation, from introductory and foundations courses to student teaching and professional development experiences.

— *Technology should be introduced in context*: Teaching pre-service students basic computer literacy-the traditional operating system, word process or, spreadsheet, database, and telecommunications topics is not enough. As with any profession, there is a level of literacy beyond general computer literacy. This more specific or professional literacy involves learning to use technology to foster the educational growth of students.

— *Professional literacy is best learned in context*: Pre-service students should learn many uses of technology because they are integrated into their coursework and field experiences. They should see their professors and mentor teachers model innovative uses of technology; they should use it in their own learning, and they should explore creative uses of technology in their teaching.

Students should experience innovative technology-supported learning environments in their teacher education programme. Technology can be used to support traditional forms of learning as well as to transform learning. A PowerPoint presentation, for example, can enhance a traditional lecture, but it does not necessarily transform the learning experience.

On the other hand, using multimedia cases to teach topics that have previously been addressed through lectures may well be an example of a learning experience transformed by technology.

Students should experience both types of uses of technology in their programme; however, the brightest promise of technology in education is as a support for new, innovative, and creative forms of teaching and learning. While the proposed ICT in teacher education curriculum should aspire to no less, the trajectory of the development for countries, regions, and organizations should be appropriate to the level of resources, including expertise, leadership, and ICTs themselves.

A widespread approach to reach a scattered population of teachers and organizations that are ready to move a small step forward with very limited resources may be helpful at an early stage.

Creating centres of transferable excellent practice that encourage 'reference site ' visits, and mentoring teachers in other locations, are also approaches that may be effective.

Since there are a variety of approaches, an overview of the many stages in which teachers receive teacher education may prove helpful. Professional development to incorporate ICTs into teaching and learning is an ongoing process and should not be thought of as one 'injection' of training. Teachers need to update their knowledge and skills as the school curriculum and technologies change.

Individuals develop in stages and mature over time. Personal development must be accompanied by organizational development in schools, training centres, and universities. In many regions, teachers engage in preparation before they start teaching in schools.

When pre-service teachers begin to teach they may be given additional support to handle the complexity of their work for the first to third years of their career. This stage of professional development is called induction. The induction stage demands a great deal of effort and commitment, and research in developed countries reveals that around 30% of teachers may drop out during this time.

Some teachers do not have the benefit of a preparatory course and must learn while teaching in schools, a condition referred to as on-the-job training. Such training is probably carried out within the school, perhaps with the teacher receiving some release from normal duties.

Teacher education is an ongoing process of lifelong learning. The final stage, consisting of additional professional development, is called in-service teacher education. It is important to note that some very strong models of teacher education provide simultaneous professional development for more than one group.

For example, pre-service preparation can be aligned with in-service teacher education. A practising teacher may work with a pre-service teacher education student on an innovative educational project. This not only increases the research potential of the in-service teacher, but the pre-service teacher also experiences role modelling and, as a result, may have an easier transition into teaching.

Professional learning communities allow teachers to support the professional development of colleagues and receive support themselves. ICTs have increased the access to and reach of such professional associations. Mentorship can be fostered across geographic distances and supported by synchronous and asynchronous interaction.

Professional development may also be enhanced by public or private partnerships with the community. Such partnerships may be particularly appropriate for professional development related to ICTs, with financial and technical support contributed by ICT companies, such as the Intel Teach to the Future Programme, or by local communities.

The professional development of teacher educators is also essential. Unless teacher educators model effective use of technology in their own classes, it will not be possible to prepare a new generation of teachers who effectively use the new tools for learning. It is also important to consider the question of who may teach.

With ICTs, students often become teachers, using the processes of peer tutoring or reciprocal mentoring. Indeed, a teacher may facilitate learning by reversing the teaching-learning roles, with students acting as expert learners who model the learning process.

ICTs provide extensive opportunities for this to occur in ways that can increase the self-esteem, motivation, and engagement of students. Teachers need encouragement to adopt such strategies rather than to feel ashamed to be taught by young learners. Members of the community also may become teachers, or at least invited experts.

ICTs extend the range of such opportunities and provide access to extensive relevant supporting materials.The teacher's role changes to manager and facilitator in many of these situations as the teacher helps the expert communicate with the learners and scaffolds the learning process.

The teacher also acquires professional development by learning from the expert. The focus of professional development should also be expanded to those who work with teachers: the classroom assistants, school leaders, and members of regional and national organizations for curriculum and professional development.

A common vision for the role of ICTs in education is important for its success. Teachers may find it impossible to incorporate ICTs into their work without support and encouragement from colleagues, parents, and leaders. To bring this about, these community members may also need professional development, along with the teachers.

The most obvious technique for professional development for teachers is to provide courses in basic ICTs knowledge and skills, delivered by experts in national and regional centres. These types of courses, taught at training centres or universities with a syllabus set by regional or national agencies, have been a common practice in many countries.

However, this approach has had limited success without follow-on training and support, as compared to effective use of ICTs by trained teachers. Similarly, courses for teachers in particular software and hardware applications are difficult to implement in a way that results in use of these applications in classroom instruction or other professional practices without additional support.

The development of ICTs does not improve education if the focus is on ICTs. The vision must focus on what ICTs can do to improve education. A more successful approach is to provide on-site training in schools that addresses the concerns of individual teachers and is supported by leadership within the school.

In UK, ICT resources and an opportunity to work alongside classroom teachers. The advisory teachers were able to see the context in which the teachers worked and, with the teachers, were able to develop appropriate deployment of ICTs for curriculum use and promote the successful organization of resources in the school and the region.

This approach, however, is resource-intensive and is not feasible for many schools. Over the last decade, many countries that included ICTs in education were slow to also include it in teacher education. Only recently have national agencies begun to realize the importance of educating teachers at the beginning of their careers.

Younger people are more likely to be familiar with ICTs, to be adaptable, and to not yet have formed habitual modes of instruction that are more difficult to change with more experienced teachers. It is in the pre-serv-ice stage that they are most open to learning how to infuse technology into instruction. Based on their long experiences with traditional modes of learning, teacher educators may find it challenging to incorporate ICTs into their own instructional practices. They may also lack experience in developing the complex partnerships between higher education and schools that facilitate technology-rich contexts for training student teachers.

To bring this about, it is usually necessary that the faculty be held accountable to standards and that the institution provides both incentives and resources to support technology-rich programmes and initiatives.

One approach that encourages collaboration between the teacher preparation programme and the community is the formation of computer clubs for students interested in computers and education. This approach was used successfully in Russia and works well where computing resources are limited. Care must be taken, however to ensure that the emphasis is on education rather than on games or competitions.

Peer tutoring models are very effective in club settings and may develop into reciprocal mentoring with teachers in which the students provide ICT training for peers and teachers and the teachers mentor the tutors ' developing skills as teachers.

Peer tutoring is a relatively common approach in classrooms of cultures around the world. This approach is effective even when teachers have little ICT skill and knowledge. Parents and other community members may also serve as teachers, tutors, and co-learners, and the whole community may benefit economically because of an increase in the ICT skills among diverse members of the community.

ICTs may also support effective professional development of teachers in to how to use ICTs. A limited initiative to integrate an innovative approach to teaching and learning with one new technology for a large population of teachers can be an important early step for a nationwide strategy.

The UNESCO document, Teacher Education Through Distance Learning, describes interactive radio, a professional development model in which radio programmes provide daily half-hour lessons introducing pupils to English through active learning experiences with native English speakers.

The radio programmes reach 11,000 teachers across South Africa. The initiative is successful in developing teachers ' pedagogical, language, and technology skills. Much of this success is due to the appropriateness of the technology choice for South Africa.

When ICTs are introduced into a community, they may address multiple goals and may expand our conception of education. For example, the Drik project in Bangladesh started as an ecology project. The goal was to plant trees and educate the local population in how to care for them. The project brought a single computer with an Internet link into the community. The introduction of this computer, coupled with peer tutoring, resulted in the development of considerable ICT skills in the young people of the region, and today the school is a centre for ICT services both locally and globally.

Although the teachers were not the leaders in this initiative, they learned to adopt ICTs and incorporate them into the curriculum and administration of their school. This extension of the 'business ' of the school beyond traditional education tasks is not unusual for schools in economically depressed communities that learn the value of technology in enhancing vocational opportunities.

MirandaNet is an important example of teachers who use ICTs to mentor each other and to establish new communities connected through the Internet. The brainchild of an active teacher educator and consultant, MirandaNet is supported by partners in business and commerce. Originating in the UK, MirandaNet has spawned related communities in the Czech Republic and Chile, and negotiations are underway for a Chinese MirandaNet.

The MATEN European project provided expertise to a Ukrainian Centre which created a course for English teachers who wanted to teach through the Internet. The technology focus was on online learning and teaching. Challenges included retention of the very limited population of English teacher educators and their access to reliable Internet workstations. Despite this, the enthusiasm of a small percentage of teachers over a vast area of the former Soviet Union did result in ICT teacher education for an important cadre of teachers.

The situation may improve, as technology facilities improve and curriculum resources increase due to grants from European countries and the USA, especially for teachers of English.

This chapter mainly provides a holistic framework to assist in designing the integration of information and communication technologies (ICTs) into teacher education. The framework is coherent with the context provided by today's society and reflects more recent understandings of the nature of learning, including aspects of learning communities during the school years and beyond into life-long learning.

The holistic framework will help teacher educators and administrators consider the cultural and educational system context, technology resources, and other factors that are important in planning the integration of technology into the pre-service curriculum. Limited technology resources and conditions of rapid change in educational, economic and political systems challenge many contexts of this curriculum.

In some regions, the shortage of teachers, teacher educators, facilities and standards has been chronic for years and has reached crisis proportions. Access to ICT resources may also be quite limited.

The framework was designed by representatives of international projects to assist policy makers, course developers, teacher educators, and other professionals who are charged with developing the use of information and communication technologies (ICT) in teacher education. The model will help assure that national and local infrastructure, culture and context, among other factors, will be considered in designing new curricula, and that curricula will be kept up to date, as new developments are forged in education and ICTs.

The curriculum framework also suggests that each teacher is allowed to interpret the framework within his or her context and personal approach to pedagogy, which is always related to the subject discipline or content area, rather than to the technology itself. The four themes that bind the curriculum as a whole are described briefly below, followed by descriptions of the four core competencies.

Context and Culture identifies the culture and other contextual factors that must be considered in infusing technology into teacher education curriculum. It includes the use of technology in culturally appropriate ways and the development of respect for multiple cultures and contexts, which need to be taught and modelled by teachers.

Leadership and Vision are essential for the successful planning and implementation of technology into teacher education and require both leadership and support from the administration of the teacher education institution.

Lifelong Learning acknowledges that learning does not stop after school. In common with the other themes, it is important that teachers and teacher preparation faculty model lifelong learning as a key part of implementation, and as an ongoing commitment to ICTs in teacher education.

Planning and Management of Change is the final theme, born of today's context and accelerated by technology itself. It signifies the importance of careful planning and effective management of the change process. These themes may be understood as a strategic combination of approaches that help teacher educators develop the four core competencies.

The core competencies may be seen as clusters of objectives that are critical for successful use of ICTs as tools for learning. The ICT competencies are organized into four groups. Pedagogy is focused on teachers ' instructional practices and knowledge of the curriculum and requires that they develop applications within their disciplines that make effective use of ICTs to support and extend teaching and learning.

Collaboration and Networking acknowledges that the communicative potential of ICTs to extend learning beyond the classroom walls and the implications for teachers development of new knowledge and skills.

Technology brings with it new rights and responsibilities, including equitable access to technology resources, care for individual health, and respect for intellectual property included within the Social Issues aspect of ICT competence.

Finally, Technical Issues is an aspect of the Lifelong Learning theme through which teachers update skills with hardware and software as new generations of technology emerge. As a final reminder of the holistic nature of this curriculum, the model illustrates the interdependence of the themes and competencies—all themes interacting with all competencies.

The most important aspect of infusing technology in the curriculum is pedagogy. When implementing the pedagogical competencies for infusing technology, the local context and the individual approach of the teacher linked with that of their subject discipline must be paramount.

Teachers move through stages as they adopt ICTs. Initially, the teacher adopting technology applies it simply as a substitute for current teaching practice where technology is not used.

The adaptation of ICTs by teachers should (and does) challenge and support changes in teaching practice, building upon individual pedagogic expertise. As teachers ' pedagogical practices with new technologies continue to develop, and organizational support and access to ICTs grow, it becomes possible to move beyond the adaptation of ICT applications that fit with existing practice.

In short, as professional teachers educators continually develop their pedagogical use of ICTs to support learning, teaching, and curriculum development, including assessment of learners and the evaluation of teaching, they will:

— demonstrate understanding of the opportunities and implications of the uses of ICTs for learning and teaching in the curriculum context;

— plan, implement, and manage learning and teaching in open and flexible learning environments;

— assess and evaluate learning and teaching in open and flexible learning environments.

ICTs provide powerful new tools to support communication between learning groups and beyond classrooms. The teacher's role expands to that of a facilitator of collaboration and networking with local and global communities. The expansion of the learning community beyond the classroom also requires respect for diversity, including inter-cultural education, and equitable access to electronic learning resources.

There is growing evidence that communities learn through collaborative activities that reflect diverse cultures in authentic projects that serve society. The development of teachers' competencies in networking and collaboration are therefore essential to ICTs in education.

Through collaboration and networking, professional teachers promote democratic learning within the classroom and draw upon expertise both locally and globally. In this process, they will:

— demonstrate a critical understanding of the added value of learning networks and collaboration within and between communities and countries;

— participate effectively in open and flexible learning environments as a learner and as a teacher;

— create or develop learning networks that bring added value to the education profession and society (locally and globally); and

— widen access and provide learning opportunities to all diverse members of the community, including those with special needs.

The power to access information and communication technologies brings increased responsibilities for everyone. Legal and moral codes need to be extended to respect the intellectual property of freely accessible information. Copyright applies to web resources, too, regardless of the ability of the user to purchase the rights. This respect can be modelled in classroom practice with students from an early stage.

The challenges faced by society, locally and globally, by adoption of technology should become part of the curriculum in a way that involves learners and helps them to develop an effective voice in the debates. Health issues of ICTs also need to be addressed.

For example, prolonged engagement with ICTs requires appropriate support for the body, especially the hands and back. Similarly, hazards of electricity and other power sources require care and the modelling of safe practice. The technology standards for students and teachers from the International Society for Technology in Education (ISTE) offer guidelines for social issues, under the topic of social, ethical, legal, and human guidelines relating to the responsible use of technology.

In short, professional teachers need to understand social and health issues surrounding ICTs and apply that understanding in their practice. Specifically, they need to:

— understand and apply the legal and moral codes of practice, including copyright and respect for intellectual property;

— reflect upon and lead discussion of the impact of new technology on society, locally and globally; and

— plan and promote healthy use of ICTs, including seating, light, sound, and related energy sources (including electricity and radio signals).

Technical issues regarding integration of ICTs into the curriculum include the technical competencies and provision of both technical infrastructure and technical support for technology use throughout the curriculum.

Technical competencies of the individual are perhaps the most obvious but perhaps the least important in the long-term because use of technology should ultimately become transparent. When technology is robust and used competently, it moves from the foreground to the background and remains essential. This is similar to the process of gaining any new skillset, such as riding a bicycle.

Each new skill must be consciously attended to and practiced until it becomes an automatic response. Competent bike riders do not focus on balance and the pedals of the bike, they focus on navigation and safety. However, we do recognize that in many contexts, the lack of technology competence, infrastructure, and technical support can create barriers to access and reliability resulting in diminished support for the curriculum. Additional technical support or training is therefore advised, depending on local circumstances. Simply providing the technology for learners and teachers is not enough. The type and level of access is also important.

ICTs will improve learning very little if teachers and students have only rare and occasional access to the tools for learning. Reasonable access to ICTs has been shown to be important for the acquisition of competence with hardware and software, especially for teachers. For example, provision of portable computers is an important strategy for ICTs teacher education.

Teachers with portable computers can use them for both teaching in school and for other professional activities elsewhere. In short, professional teachers, provided with reliable technology infrastructure and technical assistance, demonstrate continual growth in their skill with ICTs and knowledge of their current and emerging applications within education and local and global society. Specifically they are able to:

— use and select from a range of ICT resources to enhance personal and professional effectiveness; and

— willingly update skills and knowledge in the light of new developments.

# 3

# Planning and Development of Teacher Education

Many regions and countries in Europe, the USA, Asia, and Australia have adopted a set of ICT standards for pre-service and in-service teacher education. A vision for ICTs in Education often precedes the development of standards. One illustrative example is the Singapore government's Master Plan for Information Technology (IT) in Education, launched in 1997 to usher in a new era of educational development. It specified three goals:

— To train every teacher in purposeful use of IT for teaching;

— To equip teachers with core skills in teaching with IT; and

— To involve institutions of higher education and industry partners in schools.

In Singapore, the National Institute for Education (NIE) is the only provider of pre-service teacher education. NIE's approach includes several notable strategies:

— It provides a short foundation course that focuses on hands-on IT experience as the initial stage of pre-service training.

— It provides more advanced IT courses as electives for students who need or want to develop more advanced IT-based pedagogical skills.

— It integrates IT components into all of the subject matter areas such as math, social studies, English, and so on, so that students have a role-model for IT-integrated teaching and learning.

— It designs IT-integrated courses in such a way that students have the opportunity to produce IT-based instructional materials themselves and share outcomes of the course with others.

The International Society for Technology in Education (ISTE) has developed a set of standards to provide guidance and consistency to programmes. These standards are used widely in several countries and serve as the National Educational Technology Standards (NETS) for the United States of America.

The ISTE NETS for Students describe what students from preschool to grade twelve should know about and be able to do with technology. The student standards provide a basis for the development of technology standards for teachers and technology standards for educational administrators. These sets of standards provide states, districts, schools, and teacher education institutions the foundations upon which the integration of technology in their programmes can be built.

Other countries and regions that have developed, adopted, or adapted national or regional standards include: Australia, China, Ireland, Latin America and the

United Kingdom. Whether a university is establishing a new teacher education programme specializing in ICT leadership or redesigning an existing teacher education programme into which technology is to be woven, ICT standards can provide a substantial foundation for the planning process.

ISTE's performance-based standards describe what the teacher candidates should do to demonstrate that they are competent users of ICTs and that they can facilitate competent use of technology by their students. In US, the ISTE National Educational Technology Standards for Teachers, provides standards and performance indicators describing what pre-service teachers should know about and be able to do with technology upon completion of their teacher preparation programme.

The rapid infusion of technology into schools requires a new generation of leaders who are able to use the new tools to enhance their own productivity and decision-making activities and who understand the importance of integrating technology into the learning process.

Leadership is often the most important factor in the successful integration of ICTs into the school's instructional practices and curriculum. Research has shown that without effective and supportive leadership, changes in the teaching-learning process and widespread, effective uses of technology in learning are not likely to occur.

To encourage educators to prepare for positions of leadership in ICTs, the ISTE Accreditation and Professional Standards Committee has developed accreditation standards for teacher preparation programmes for specialization in ICTs.

The technology specialization guidelines have been adopted by the National Council for Accreditation of Teacher Education (NCATE) and are currently used in evaluation of teacher preparation programmes for accreditation. The documented importance of a shared vision among the multiple levels of an organization indicates the need for technology standards for education administrators.

ISTE managed the development of Technology Standards for School Administrators (TSSA), which identify performance standards for the technology skills, knowledge, and dispositions of education administrators.

The TSSA Collaborative has developed standards for school administrators that include specific indicators for the superintendent, school administrator, and district level administrator. School administrators must understand and support the use of technology at all levels so that they can work collaboratively with universities on appropriate field placements and help new teachers incorporate technology into classroom instruction.

Many countries in Europe have official recommendations for ICT-related skills for future and practicing teachers. Eurydice, the information network on education in Europe, annually publishes Basic Indicators on the Incorporation of ICT into European Education Systems.

In the majority of European countries, as much importance is attached to the teachers ' personal command of ICTs as to mastery of ICTs for teaching purposes. In France, the Netherlands and the United Kingdom, the content of training is determined to some extent by the mandatory standards. In the UK, there is also a detailed curriculum for the use of ICTs in teaching specific subjects. Countries and regions adopting standards for the first time may wish to do so in stages. This was the strategy taken by the UK, which currently has the most detailed standards of any country in Europe.

The standards were first imposed with a relatively simple section within the mandatory standards (criteria for government approval of courses) for pre-service teachers in 1989. This section states: On completion of their course, all students should be able to select and make appropriate use of a range of equipment and resources to promote learning.

In particular, all courses should contain compulsory and clearly identifiable elements that enable students to make effective use of information technology (IT) in the classroom and provide a sound basis for their subsequent development in the field. They should be trained to:

— make confident personal use of a range of software packages and IT devices appropriate to their subject specialization and age range;

— review critically the relevance of software packages and IT devices to their subject specialization and age range and judge the potential value of these in classroom use;

— make constructive use of IT in their teaching and in particular prepare and put into effect schemes of work incorporating appropriate uses of IT; and

— evaluate the ways in which the use of IT changes the nature of teaching and learning.

Some years later the UK government developed highly detailed standards for pre-service teacher education and then also developed a nationwide strategy to train all teachers in pedagogical use of ICTs. The detailed curriculum has the following expected outcomes for teachers. Teachers should know:

— when, when not and how to use ICTs in teaching their subject;

— how ICTs can be used for teaching the whole class;

— how ICTs can be used when planning, including the use of ICTs for lesson preparation and the choice and organization of ICT resources;

— how to assess pupils' work when ICTs have been used; and

— how ICTs can be used to keep up-to-date, share best practice and reduce bureaucracy.

The Teacher Training Agency also developed a CD to help teachers analyze their own training needs. A complementary outcomes-based curriculum has also been developed for school librarians. An ICT training initiative funded by a charitable lottery has resulted in the creation of a large number of training organizations, many of which are public-private partnerships.

A different approach has been taken in Scandinavia. A standard test was first developed that focused on ICT skills. It is known as the European Computer Driving License (ECDL) and is used in many professions and with students in schools. More recently, a Pedagogical ICT Driving License has been developed for primary and secondary school teachers in Denmark for the integration of ICTs in education.

Several countries in South America have extensive projects to develop and integrate ICTs in education, but the lack of national policies for the use of ICTs is notable. The final example provided is the generic curriculum used by the international Intel Applying Computers in Education (ACE) project. The project trains classroom teachers to integrate the use of computers into existing curriculum to increase student learning and achievement. Originated in the USA in 1998, it is now in operation in several countries. The curriculum is summarized by these themes of training:

— Using computers and learning and productivity tools for both teachers and students.

— Using the types of computers and software that are widely available in both schools and industry.

— An emphasis on "hands-on" learning and the creation of lessons which teachers can effectively use in their classrooms.

— Encouraging teachers to work in teams, problem-solve and participate in peer-review of their lessons.

## ICT Curriculum for Teacher Education

A first step in determining the ICT curriculum for a university teacher education programme is to examine the expectations identified in the ICT standards for students, or standards for teachers aligned with the student standards. Through the ongoing use of technology in the schooling process, students should achieve important technology capabilities.

The key individual in helping students achieve those capabilities is the classroom teacher. The teacher is responsible for establishing the classroom environment and preparing the learning opportunities that facilitate students ' use of technology to learn, communicate, and develop knowledge products; consequently, it is critical that all classroom teachers are prepared to provide their students with these opportunities.

Teacher preparation programmes must provide technology-rich experiences throughout all aspects of the training programmes. Teachers must be prepared to empower students with the advantages technology can bring. Schools and classrooms, both real and virtual, must have teachers who are equipped with technology resources and skills and who can effectively teach the necessary subject matter content while incorporating technology concepts and skills.

Real-world connections, primary source materials, and sophisticated data-gathering and analysis tools are only a few of the resources that allow teachers to provide heretofore unimaginable opportunities for developing their students' conceptual understandings. Traditional educational practices no longer provide pre-service teachers with the skills necessary to teach students to survive economically in today's workplace.

Teachers must prepare their students to apply strategies for problem solving, and to use appropriate tools for learning, calculating, collaborating, and communicating. ICT tools and resources can contribute dramatically to establishing these new learning environments, both in P-12 schools and in colleges of education. ICT competencies must be integrated into the curricular and pedagogical content presented, preparing teacher candidates to create the new learning environments.

Teacher educators must therefore model the use of these new learning environments in their own university classrooms. The curriculum for teacher educators is often rich with strategies for presenting subject matter and pedagogy; however, it may be lean in terms of integrating technological tools for supporting that learning.

Consequently, curriculum developers for teacher preparation programmes must be vigilant in identifying appropriate ways to apply ICT tools throughout the coursework and experiences planned for pre-service teachers.

In an effort to implement ICT standards in a variety of coursework taken by pre-service teachers across all subject disciplines, a number of methods and strategies have been identified. Many of these strategies employ commonly used productivity tools such as word processing, database, spreadsheet, or browser applications. These software tools can be used in countless ways to support the subject area curricula.

A WebQuest is an inquiry-oriented activity in which most or all of the information used by learners is drawn from the Web. WebQuests are designed to use learners ' time well, to focus on using information rather than looking for it; and to support learners ' thinking at the levels of analysis, synthesis, and evaluation.

The WebQuest model has been effectively applied to all levels of education, from elementary to postgraduate study, and in many different subject Areas. The WebQuest provides teachers an option of reviewing and selecting web-based learning activities in a lesson-type format.

The WebQuest model encourages teachers to create for their students new activities and adapt successful ones to take advantage of the Web's power. A high-er-level application of this model has students develop their own Web-Quest activities to support the subject matter they are studying, and share the WebQuests with their peers.

CyberGuides include standards-based, web-delivered units of instruction centred on core works of literature. CyberGuides provide a quick supplementary set of activities for students as they explore specific pieces of literature. Each CyberGuide contains a student and teacher edition, targeted standards, a description of the task, a process by which the task may be completed, teacher-selected web sites, and an assessment rubric.

The teacher's guide includes an overview of the activities, suggestions from the author, and a library of links. The student guides include activity directions written in a format appropriate for the age and reading ability of the students.

Multimedia combines media objects such as text, graphics, video, animation, and sound to represent and convey information. In this project-based method of teaching and learning, students acquire new knowledge and skills by designing, planning, and producing a multimedia product. Many teachers find that students are motivated to learn when they can use technology to present the results of a rich project or activity.

The multimedia presentation contains content conveyed by the student's selection of media. The teachers in training can look at examples of projects and lessons, at Internet sites housing collections of student samples. Some examples of multimedia presentations include:

— creating a web page or site;

— developing a branching hypermedia stack;

— using a multimedia slide show application to create a computer presentation;

— shooting and editing video to create a computer-generated movie.

Multimedia-authoring tools are used to link and branch screens, making them interactive and layered with information in photos, scanned images, movies, and text. Students and candidates can easily narrate their projects using a microphone.

Telecomputing projects are Internet-enriched learning activities that often involve students in one location collaborating with students or adults in one or more other locations. They may share, among other things:

— experiences

— beliefs

— data

— information

— problem-solving strategies

— products they have developed or jointly developed.

Telecomputing tools include email, electronic mailing lists, electronic bulletin boards, discussion groups, web browsers, real-time chatting, and audio-and video-conferencing.

## Online Resources for Teacher Education

Online resources include web sites, interactive environments, and remotely operated robotic devices. A common type of telecomputing activity is online discussion. With the growth of infrastructure around the world comes the ability to access others through remote connections. Students and teacher candidates can connect to experts and peers through a variety of formats, such as chat rooms, electronic bulletin boards, and email.

Communicating online offers participants freedom to send and receive information efficiently across diverse geographic locations. Communication can occur asynchronously allowing time for reflection, or to compensate for varying time zones. In real-time online communication, as in chat groups, the communication is synchronous and provides immediate feedback for reinforcement and understanding.

Online discussions can provide rich learning experiences as the inter-cultural exchanges develop both linguistic skills and cultural knowledge. One successful strategy is for students to read in the target language, while writing in their native language. The Three Pomegranate Network of Armenian provides an excellent example of connecting a society in Diaspora-almost two thirds of Armenians live outside their contemporary homeland. The project links different Armenian schools across the world, each with varying degrees of access to technology and training, but all wishing to strengthen their awareness of a shared personal heritage, including the Armenian language and alphabet.

The ICT curriculum for Armenian teachers is project-based and structured around a task, such as the production of a web-based newsletter. The project provides valuable strategies for the planning of curriculum across cultures and schools, which are summarized as follows:

— *Language: Instructions* and other input from the project designers are bilingual. Students work in the target language, Armenian in this case. Software has been developed to include the target language alphabet.

— *Points of contact* :Schools serving Armenian children are linked electronically to schools in Armenia in the collaborative projects. Home and community centres need careful development to act as coordinating centres for curriculum projects.

— *Informal catalyst* :An informal catalyst to collaboration is necessary. In this project, the school in Armenia always takes this role.

— *Community building*: the projects, exercise and games are specially designed for the Diaspora, including activities that introduce students new to their culture.

— *Connectivity*: The project uses a flexible set of connectivity solutions including: direct access, connectivity centres, the Web, and CD's as a means of providing wider access.

## Quality assurance in Teacher Education

Quality assurance in teacher education is an ongoing

process and is demonstrated in a number of different ways. The teacher education institution itself may be scrutinized along with individual programmes within the institution. The quality of the teacher education institution and its programmes is often judged by the performance of the teachers they produce and the success of their graduates in effecting improved student learning in their P-12 classrooms.

Quality assurance is often determined through an accreditation process. Demonstrated competence of teacher candidates in use of ICTs in teacher education has become increasingly important in making accreditation, certification, and programme review decisions. This is particularly true in the two countries that have adopted detailed national standards, the United States and the United Kingdom. Quality assurance is uncommon in other countries, except through the evaluation of projects and strategic initiatives.

In the USA, the National Council for Accreditation of Teacher Education (NCATE) recognizes high quality university programmes through an accreditation process. NCATE provides national accreditation standards for the teacher education unit and for a variety of programmes within the unit, including those preparing candidates specializing in ICTs.

NCATE has developed a strong collaboration with the professional association, International Society for Technology in Education (ISTE). ISTE is responsible for recommending to NCATE the standards for programmes preparing Secondary Teachers of Computer Science, school-level Technology Facilitators, and Technology Directors for districts or regional areas. ISTE is also responsible for reviewing the NCATE Programme

Reports from universities seeking national recognition for their ICT programmes.

The ISTE affiliation with NCATE has resulted in strong accreditation guidelines for technology in teacher preparation programmes, as well as programmes preparing individuals for leadership roles in planning and implementing ICTs in educational environments.

Guidelines are also in place identifying the requirements for technology integration throughout teacher preparation programmes, as required by the new performance-based NCATE Standards adopted in May 2000. In their institutional report, each unit, or college of education, seeking initial accreditation is required to submit its conceptual framework outlining the philosophical and pedagogical underpinnings of the programme as a precondition for NCATE accreditation eligibility.

## Professional Development for Teacher Education

The most critical factor in the successful integration of ICTs into teacher education is the extent to which the teacher educators have the knowledge and skills for modelling the use of ICTs in their own teaching practices. To enable them to develop these skills requires a well-conceived and sustained programme of professional development.

Countries that have initiated efforts to infuse ICTs into teacher education have found four professional development strategies helpful in successful technology integration.

First, professional development needs to focus on teaching and learning rather than on hardware and software. It should be designed by first considering what student teachers are expected to know and be able to do in a specific discipline, and then infusing ICTs into the learning process so that acquiring the knowledge and skills is more efficient.

Second, professional development is practically useless unless leaders and teacher educators are provided with access to technology resources and have the time and support-when needed - to apply the new knowledge and skills that they have learned. A just-in-time approach to professional development is a model that works well. In this approach, professional development is provided to teacher educators when they have a need or opportunity to use a specific technology tool or application to enhance learning.

Third, professional development in the use of ICTs is not a one-time activity. To keep current with new developments means that professional development in ICTs must be an ongoing process.

A further strategy for professional development is to start in a small way. Start by providing professional development in the use of ICTs to a small group of teaching staff. Perhaps this group will have volunteered or demonstrated that they have basic ICT competencies for personal use, or have expressed personal interest in using ICTs in their teaching. Working with this small group allows the professional development staff to determine the specific interests and needs of the teacher educators and what works best in the professional development process.

Professional development may be provided to other small groups of faculty, thus expanding and refining the professional development efforts. The most important criterion for effective professional development is to tailor it to the learning needs and skill levels of individual teaching staff within a faculty. This suggests that, ideally, an institution should, based on availability of resources, provide a variety of options for professional development for the faculty.

In structuring professional development options and resources, it is helpful to explore collaboration opportunities with partners outside the university. The opportunities for ICTs to create new paradigms of teaching and learning will depend largely on leadership and a shared vision, and on appropriate and continuing professional development.

The planning and implementation of ICT-related professional development of teacher educators should be led by a planning group that includes representation and expertise from teacher educators, programme administrators, teachers, school administrators, technology experts, and business leaders.

The diverse perspectives of the group should provide an understanding of the realities of the classroom, new views of the teaching-learning process, knowledge of the array of technologies that may be used to enhance learning, and community opinions. It is important for a planning group to negotiate a shared understanding of the role of ICTs in the agenda for educational renewal based on their individual cares and concerns.

It is also helpful to have a larger advisory or liaison group that may facilitate collaborative professional development efforts and sharing of resources across related organizations, for example, between the university and the partner schools where students are placed for teaching practice. An important aspect of professional development is not only enabling teacher educators to understand and use ICT tools in their teaching practices, but understanding how technology coupled with new approaches to teaching and learning, may enhance student learning.

Many teacher educators recognize that approaches to education are changing and that new technology has the potential to improve education and student learning. They may also recognize the implications of increasing use of technology in society and employment, including employment directly related to their own disciplines and content areas. Less obvious are the implications for literacy and numeracy at the core of the educational process, and the need for teacher educators themselves to model good practice in their teaching so that their students can easily transfer these strategies into their own teaching practice.

Teacher educators are experts in a domain, and it is important to respect this domain while helping them to revitalize and modernize their teaching with ICTs. Similarly, the risk that established teacher educators must take to develop their practice needs to be recognized and mitigated as much as possible.

The most significant change required of individuals and organizations providing teacher education is to redefine student roles and responsibilities. Both students and teachers have always had rights and responsibilities, but the redefinition of the learning environment requires a change in the balance of rights and responsibilities, with the student assuming more of both.

ICTs demand this shift because technologies are constantly changing. Students need to develop the ability to think for themselves, continually learn as technologies change, and provide support to one another. This last element, peer teaching, is a natural product of ICTs because often the younger generations bring increasingly high levels of competence into the learning environment. This is a positive shift, and it should be noted that these strategies are also appropriate for competencies that do not involve ICTs.

## Development Stages for ICT

Teachers and teacher educators develop ICT competence in stages. Those who are fluent with technology may not appreciate how difficult it is for technology novices to appropriate ICTs into their professional practice. Teacher educators often find this task even more difficult than teachers do, because they typically have higher levels of content and pedagogical expertise that must be respected.

Teacher educators, because they have to work in multiple contexts-both the home institution and the field where students are placed to observe and practice teaching-may also be more influenced by the absence of the essential conditions for ICTs in teacher education.

Four stages are common, but they may be repeated with new forms of ICTs or applications of ICTs to new areas. The first stage for each individual is awareness, and the appropriate response at this stage is to provide information about a relevant application of ICTs and appropriate ways that it may be used in the individual's current professional or personal concerns.

Teacher educators then explore the use of the application. They need support to put this ICT application into practice in a timely manner and to reflect on its effectiveness. Only after teacher educators have gone through these stages are they able to adapt their practice to make better use of ICTs, and then move toward the final stage to become innovators and modellers of excellent practice for their students and colleagues.

The advent of ICTs provides the opportunity to engage in this process from a new perspective and to model processes of learning for colleagues and students. It is acceptable for teacher educators to adopt only those aspects of ICTs that are relevant to their practice, but they must first be allowed to explore the range of possibilities, so that they and their students may become critically aware of, and competent in, diverse ICT applications. Of course, any teacher educators continually strive to be responsive to developments and innovations in education within and beyond their discipline.

To understand the strategies of professional development it is important to understand how they are embedded in the broader context of the planning and implementation of ICTs in teacher education.

Teacher educators need to develop competence in the core themes of: pedagogy, collaboration and networking, technical competence, and social issues. This needs to be done within the local and global cultural contexts of: lifelong learning, leadership and vision, and planning and management of change.

For example, a growing number of pre-service teacher education programmes in the USA have employed the ISTE technology standards, and ISTE describes the best of these programmes on the ISTE web site. One such programme was initiated at the University of Texas at Austin, where the teacher educators expert in ICTs have actively planned and promoted the professional development of their colleagues and facilitated the management of change.

The culture is one in which all participants respect the leadership and vision provided by the dean and the college's technology support centre. The current programme evolved from the experiences gained in working with the teacher education faculty. It underscores the importance of learning from the mistakes, as well as the successes, in implementing professional development.

For example, a faculty development workshop was held to teach faculty to use a tool to incorporate web-based elements into their teaching. An initial training session was offered that provided the faculty with an extensive demonstration of the full range of capabilities of the tool. The faculty participants left the two-hour session with cognitive overload and little that they could immediately apply to their courses. Based on this experience, another workshop was designed that focused on a few useful applications that faculty could incorporate into their instruction.

The teacher educators were asked to bring class syllabi and selected course resources to the workshop. The teacher educators learned how to post these materials online in WebCT and set up online class discussions. After the teacher educators had time to see how this worked in practice with their students, a second workshop was provided to help them consider appropriate ways to facilitate collaboration and networking, along with the social issues that might arise in using these methods. These redesigned workshops were highly successful and led to ongoing faculty development.

This effort was successful because this strategy permitted the teacher educators to gain new information about the software within a pedagogical approach that addressed their immediate concerns, and allowed them to pilot the approach and evaluate their efforts. A similar strategy works for other widely used software application tools, such as word processing and desktop publishing.

Professional development for ICTs in teacher education is ongoing, as denoted by the theme of lifelong learning. Successful models for professional development must reflect this dynamic nature by building capacity rather than teaching skills. Reciprocal mentoring is an example of a professional development model that builds capacity within an organization.

In US, Iowa State University has an award-winning programme of teacher education and supports this excellence by providing professional development in ICTs for its teacher educators and the in-service teachers who work with students. Over a decade ago, the course Technology and Teacher Education was established to provide graduate students with an internship experience.

Many of these students become teacher educators who are expert in ICTs. These students mentored teacher educators in ICT skills and, in return, the teacher educators mentored the students in their profession. The graduate students ' advisor, who strategically selected or negotiated the participation of teacher educators, facilitated and planned the interaction.

Over the years, the balance moved from encouragement of reluctant teacher educators to participate, to the strategic choice of participants from a long list of volunteers. Similarly, the context and culture became increasingly akin to a sociable family that supports one another; an organization in which members learn from one another while collaborating and networking. The mentoring course takes place in the fall semester.

Technical competence is purposefully developed slowly, to keep pace with the emerging confidence and autonomy levels of the teacher educator. The graduate students' advisor insists that mentoring graduate students assist the teacher educator to engage with ICTs, rather than allow the teacher educator to delegate the ICT tasks to the student mentor.

ICT applications used in instruction are favoured over those for research, so that the mentoring graduate student can support and experience the development of pedagogic competence. The mentor pairs are expected to engage in many rich conversations as they work together, covering diverse themes and competencies, including social issues with ICTs and discipline specific topics.

Toward the end of the semester, the teacher educators join the mentors ' class for a celebration of their collaborative professional and course development. At this time the teacher educators are exposed to a wide range of ICT applications, cultures, and contexts, and reflect on the four themes and competencies.

A number of states and regions have engaged in a renewal of education. Part of their strategy includes ICTs as a catalyst. However, ICT use is not, in itself, a useful goal. According to a study by the Organization for Economic Co-Operation and Development (OECD) (in preparation), ICTs can be viewed as neutral, i.e., they may support both effective and ineffective education. Effective plans must include strategic objectives and educational vision to inform the use of ICTs for educational renewal.

Leadership and vision are an even more important theme at this transformative level of ICT use in teacher education. Below is an eclectic mix of illustrations to inform professional development planning at the regional and national levels. The framework is used to analyze the mix of themes and competencies that may be developed by particular strategies at the regional, national and international level.

Project InTent was the first national initiative to integrate ICTs into pre-service teacher education. It took place in England between 1989 and 1992, following increasing pressure to prepare teachers before they started practising in schools. The national association of ICT teacher educators published a survey that identified the lack of resources and support for their work.

This first national programme to integrate ICTs into pre-service teacher education requested proposals. Five different types of institutions in England were selected to represent the different types of teacher education organizations. Periodic visits to each organization by the coordinator provided her opportunities to act both as a leader and a mentor for all ICT teacher educators.

An inclusive learning community developed that supported the adoption of a participative action research approach by all project participants and other stakeholders. The project established and published a special journal series called 'Developing information technology in teacher education.' In this way, the project adopted a collaborative networking approach to organizational development to integrate ICTs into teacher education, and the five institutions reinforced each other's commitment to serve the pedagogic needs of all their colleagues, regardless of discipline or approach to content.

There was never any doubt of the aim: colleagues modelling excellent practice with ICTs as they taught methods and content-specific topics. The consortium worked through technical and social issues while integrating ICTs into courses for pre-service teachers, and they supported action research analysis of their own and their colleagues ' professional development while planning and managing change.

One particularly innovative approach to support transfer into school-based practice was to bring an elementary class into the primary base at one of the universities. This practice teaching was intensively supported with lectures, equipment, software, and technical support.

All the teacher educators and support staff received ICT professional development to facilitate a rich environment of good educational practice. Students were able to practice teaching in pairs with a group of four children. This strategy may be particularly appropriate at early stages of ICT adoption in a region where there are few resources and little ICT practice in local schools.

In US, the new government requirement for ICTs in pre-service teacher education provided ample justification for change and an argument for expanding resources in teacher education. The national project leader contributed to institutional development through her research of organizational change, informed by structured interviews of strategically important people. This gathering of evidence was both action and research, because the act of interviewing prompted these people to reflect on ICTs and their place in their organization.

In 1999, educators and policy-makers in the United States recognized the growing crisis in teacher retention and recruitment. The need to develop capacity for ICTs in teacher education within universities and colleges was informed by several research studies in teacher education, undertaken by leading ICT teacher educators with support of their professional societies. It became clear that the improvement of pre-serv-ice teacher education would be an effective use of resources, particularly at a time when schools were losing a high percentage of teachers within five years.

The resources to initiatives that were already using ICTs in innovative ways to enable them to share their expertise in building capacity across a large geographic area. Some of the catalyst projects developed high-quality resources to support the infusion of ICTs into teacher education, such as multimedia case studies of ICTs in schools and universities, and software to assist reflective practice, many of which can be accessed on the Internet.

In addition, in collaboration with the only international society specializing in ICTs in teacher education, a new online journal was established to promote discussion and development, with autonomy for sections edited by relevant content areas.

In Chile, the national ICT initiative is called Enlaces .In common with all of the cited examples of good practice, the design was informed and led by ICT experts, and in this case, the team came from a leading university centre, the Instituto de Informatica Educativa of the Universidad de La Frontera.

The centre conceived the initiative and has played a central role in the development of the Enlaces programme since 1993. In conjunction with the Ministry of Education, it is responsible for the national coordination of the Enlaces Educational Network. The Institute also conducts research and development activities to support the use of information and communication technology in the network's schools.

The centre was informed by scholarly research in this area, and at least one of the ICT teacher educators undertook a doctoral degree on this topic with leading experts in the University of London Institute of Education. To inform early stages of development and ongoing evaluation the Enlaces initiative drew on a wide range of international consultants in ICTs in education, as well as this close doctoral level supervision. The majority of ICT teacher educators in Enlaces were drawn from 24 universities, which became known as the Technical Assistance Network.

This network was built upon a strategic alliance between the Ministry of Education and universities across the country. The Technical Assistance Network's mission was to train teachers and provide them with technical and educational support. Six universities, designated as Regional Centres, served as coordinators, managing Enlaces activities and teacher training in a particular geographical area of the country. They also carried out applied research in the field of educational ICTs.

One of the fundamental premises of the Enlaces programme was that merely supplying information technology to schools is not enough to bring about significant changes in the quality of education.

Although ICTs can potentially simplify and enhance the learning process in all subject areas and in some cases act as a catalyst for innovation, additional efforts such as teacher training and support -must be done in order to produce sustainable changes in pedagogical practices and student learning outcomes.

Information and communication technologies are tools to be used by all participants in the educational process: students, teachers, school administrators, parents, and sponsors; thus, great emphasis was placed on teacher training and the development of a technical assistance network.

The notions that learning computer skills is an end in itself and only experts can use ICTs were rejected. The goal is to not only equip schools with computers, but also to connect them with each other and the world through an educational network, thus enabling schools to exchange ideas and experiences regardless of their location. This goal also addresses one of the Chilean Educational Reform's key objectives: increasing equity in educational opportunity for all Chilean students.

No single formula can be applied uniformly to all schools, and the uses to which computers and networks are put will depend upon each school's educational projects, needs, and social, cultural, and geographical environment. These considerations, combined with the enthusiasm and initiative of teachers, administrators and students across the country, have often led to surprising results, with broader and deeper implications than those foreseen by the programme.

Enlaces reached 100% of the secondary schools and 50% of the primary schools by 2000, thus covering 90% of the school population. Within this group, Enlaces created an advanced group of ICT-using teachers in 51 schools from different areas of the country. The schools provided local reference sites to demonstrate ICT practice embedded in the local context and culture.

Enlaces equipped these schools with more computers, technical support, and pedagogical assistance than the regular schools, with the expectation that they would become field-based ICT teacher education sites. As a result, these schools formed the core of the collaborative professional development activities that occurred through the Internet.

Furthermore, external evaluations showed that many of the teachers believed that communications via computers in their classes had improved the quality of the teaching-learning process. Two major challenges revealed by these evaluations are the need to supply schools with more computers and a greater variety of educational software, and the concern among teachers about their heavy unpaid workload. The participating schools gained greater prestige in their communities, which translated into increases in enrolment (increased income via larger subsidies).

School officials also valued the increase in equity that occurred as a result of the project's providing equipment that schools otherwise would not have been able to acquire and the coun-try-wide spread of free access to Internet resources. The project also produced improvements in parents ' perception of their schools' performances, which facilitates the learning and teaching process.

From a more global perspective, the evaluations made by the World Bank and the Agency for International Development praise the Enlaces project as one of the most successful programmes in Chile's efforts at educational reform. An important point in this positive evaluation is that the project has expanded its coverage to the national level without sacrificing quality or equity.

Among the factors in this success, the evaluations mention the programme's focus on teachers, the construction of a social network of educators and pupils facilitated by user-friendly technology and decentralized support, and respect for participating schools ' autonomous decisions in the use of the programme's technologies.

The evaluations also emphasize the high quality of the project's technical and administrative team, which has maintained a balanced mix of a clear vision, flexibility, and creativity in the face of new educational challenges and fast-changing technology.

Intel Corporation has launched an international initiative to provide professional development resources to teacher educators in several countries. The programme is based on the Intel Teach to the Future programme begun January 2000 in the United States. The original programme provided training to in-service teachers on the integration of computer technology into teaching and learning.

University faculty who worked with this in-service programme were so impressed by the quality and depth of the pedagogy and materials that they worked with Intel to develop a version of the programme that can be used at the university level with pre-service teachers.

Since then, the materials and curricula have been adapted to thirteen different languages including Spanish, Portuguese, English (British and US), Chinese, Hindi, Japanese, Korean, Urdu (Pakistan), German, Polish, Hebrew, and Russian. As a result, the programme is currently used in teacher preparation programmes in Argentina, Brazil, Canada, China, Costa Rica, Germany, India, Ireland, Italy, Mexico, Taiwan, United Kingdom, and the United States. There are plans to use Intel Teach to the Future in eleven additional countries within the next two years.

The ultimate goal of the Intel Teach to the Future programme is to engage elementary and secondary students in culturally and pedagogically appropriate learning experiences that are enhanced by using computers. "The core focus of this curriculum is to ensure that technology is used successfully to improve student learning. "Teachers are guided to develop face-to-face, student-centred activities that model effective use of technology for teaching and learning.

The Intel Teach to the Future pre-service curricula are designed so that teacher educators and pre-service teachers can use it in a variety of learning Settings. Materials include paper and digital (CD-ROM) resources as well as Web support. Participants learn to use and integrate all three types of resources in their teaching and learning. Topics covered include:

— Developing and teaching technology-enhanced curricula

— Locating and evaluating web resources

— Copyright and citing of sources

— Designing and creating multimedia presentations, desktop-published products, and web sites

— Designing and creating teacher support materials

— Developing plans for project implementation

— Project development and assessment

For many teachers this involves a shift in approach from lecturer and expert to facilitator and learner. Examples created by participants are included with programme materials to assist other pre-service teachers as they develop their own plans and resources. Participants are encouraged to adapt these examples so that they reflect their knowledge of their own cultures. As local teachers develop new examples, they are added to the resource packet for their specific country. This adds relevance and role modelling, and encourages collaboration among pre-service teachers, their colleagues, and university faculty.

# 4

# Technology Use in Teacher Proficiency

Teacher professional development is absolutely essential if technology provided to schools is to be used effectively. Simply put, spending scarce resources on informational technology hardware and software without financing teacher professional development as well is wasteful. Experience around the world in developing, industrialized, and information-based countries has shown that teacher training in the use and application of technology is the key determining factor for improved student performance. Educational technology is not, and never will be, transformative on its own-it requires teachers who can integrate technology into the curriculum and use it to improve student learning.

In other words, computers cannot replace teachers-teachers are the key to whether technology is used appropriately and effectively. That said, designing and implementing successful teacher professional development programs in the application of technology is neither easy nor inexpensive. There are more cases of inadequate and ineffective training programs than there are success stories. Moreover, success stories are not automatically transferable to other situations, and the total body of experience and knowledge in this field is in its infancy. While some people may know more than others in this area, there are few if any true "experts." This calls for humility, innovation, a willingness to fail, ongoing evaluation, sharing of both positive and negative experiences, and constant revision of teacher professional development programmes related to technology. Even if students could learn independently how to use technology to enhance their learning and skills development, with little or no involvement from their teachers, they are highly unlikely to have those opportunities if teachers do not let them have access to technology.

Teachers remain the gatekeepers for students' access to educational opportunities afforded by technology: they cannot and should not be ignored. Moreover, providing technical skills training to teachers in the use of technology is not enough. Teachers also need professional development in the pedagogical application of those skills to improve teaching and learning. Traditional one-time teacher training workshops have not been effective in helping teachers to feel comfortable using technology or to integrate it successfully into their teaching. Instead, a new paradigm is emerging that replaces training with lifelong professional preparedness and development of teachers. This approach includes at least three dimensions are given below:

— Initial preparation/training (preservice) that provides teachers with a solid foundation of knowledge;

competency in teaching, classroom management, and organization skills; mastery of the subject matter they will teach; and proficiency in using a variety of educational resources, including technology.

— Workshops, seminars, and short courses (inservice) that offer structured opportunities for acquisition of new teaching skills and subject matter knowledge, as well as skills development in the use of technology in the classroom, that are government-certified and linked to teachers' professional career development.

— Ongoing pedagogical and technical support for teachers as they address their daily challenges and responsibilities. While technology increases teachers' training and professional development needs, it also offers part of the solution. Information and communication technologies (ICTs) can improve preservice teacher training by providing access to more and better educational resources, offering multimedia simulations of good teaching practice, catalyzing teacher-to-trainee collaboration, and increasing productivity of noninstructional tasks. ICTs also can enable inservice teacher professional development at a distance, asynchronous learning, and individualized training opportunities. Finally, ICTs can overcome teachers' isolation, breaking down their classroom walls and connecting them to colleagues, mentors, curriculum experts, and the global teacher community. This has consequences for reform of curricula, examinations, provision of educational resources, and teachers' professional development. Indeed, one of the most exciting aspects of information and communication technology is its role as a catalyst for such educational reform. The specific content of such programs is then discussed, after which the issue of teachers' motivation and incentives to participate in professional development programs related to technology is addressed.

The importance of training additional school community members is stressed, and recommendations are offered for overcoming the persistent problem of insufficient funding for teacher professional development. Next, the potential of technology as a medium for delivering teacher professional development programs is examined, followed by a discussion of future trends in teacher professional development. Most teachers want to learn to use educational technology effectively, but they lack the conceptual framework, time, computer access, and support necessary to do so.

A well-planned, ongoing professional development program, grounded in a theoretical model, linked to curricular objectives, incorporating formative evaluation activities, and sustained by sufficient financial and staff support is essential if teachers are to use technology effectively to improve student learning. When designing or implementing any teacher professional development program for technology, it is important to situate that program within the context of a theoretical framework for adult learning. Each of the dimensions is presented as a continuum, with contrasting values at either end. Teacher professional development in the use of technology should be designed and implemented to move teachers (and, eventually, students) toward the right-hand end of this continuum.

This framework emphasizes the potential of Web-based instruction to contribute to pedagogical reform, rather than technology's rich multimedia features or its ability to access information resources around the world. Stated more simply, technology can promote effective instruction that is more student-centered, interdisciplinary, more closely related to real-life events and processes, and adaptive to individual learning styles. Such instruction encourages development of higher-order thinking and information-reasoning skills (rather than memorization of facts) among students, and socially constructed (collaborative) learning, all of which are increasingly required in today's knowledge-based global economy. This potential of technology to improve instruction needs to be integrated (modeled) into the design and delivery of teacher professional development programs in the use of technology. Perhaps most important for the purpose of teachers' professional development, technology implies a shift in the teacher's role from being the sole source of knowledge and instruction to being a facilitator of students' learning, which is acquired from many sources. This is often referred to as a shift from being "the sage on the stage to the guide on the side." Again, teacher professional development for ICTs needs to incorporate and model this shift. Failure to incorporate these 10 dimensions of interactive learning into teacher professional development programs in the use and integration of technology will cripple the potential of technology to improve teaching and learning. This implies that teacher professional development in the use of technology should embody and model the forms of pedagogy that teachers can use in their classrooms. For example, these training programs should accomplish the following:

- Empower teachers to develop their knowledge and skills actively and experientially, in a variety of learning environments, both individual and collaborative.

— Include a variety of learning strategies, encompassing direct instruction, deduction, discussion, drill and practice, deduction, induction, and sharing.

— Aim at higher-order thinking skills.

— Provide an authentic learning environment so that teachers engage in concrete tasks within realistic scenarios.

— Emphasize ways that technology can facilitate and enhance teachers' professional lives.

— Encourage teachers to be mentors, tutors, and guides of the students' learning process

— Develop teachers' skills in learning how to learn

— Promote cooperative and collaborative learning.

— Be sensitive to the culture and diversity of teachers as learners, using a multifaceted approach to respond to different learning styles, opportunities, environments, and starting points.

— Enable learning independent of time and place.

More concretely, this means that teacher professional development in the use of technology needs to combine lecture/ presentation modalities with small-group and plenary discussion, individual and collaborative activities, and opportunities for teachers to reflect on their actual teaching practices and how they might do things differently with technology. Such an approach also means that learning materials need to be in several formats: print, CD-ROM, e-mail attachments, online (HTML and Java), and even DVD. It also implies a need to develop both synchronous and asynchronous modalities, so that teachers can take advantage of training opportunities when they have the time, which is not necessarily when the trainer is available.

Key to successful teacher professional development programs is a modular structure, corresponding to different levels of teacher experience and expertise using technology. Adapting materials to teachers' comfort level and starting points is essential. In this way, teachers new to technology can be exposed to the full series of professional development modules, while those further along on the learning curve can enter where their knowledge and skills stop, and help their less technology-savvy colleagues along. The basic principles of adult learning also should be incorporated into the training program. This implies that the program should be highly social and cooperative, with opportunities to share experiences and combine instruction with discussion, reflection, application, and evaluation.

In addition to these principles, technology enables an even more collaborative approach and maximizes peer-to-peer sharing of the challenges, frustrations, advantages, and successes of using technology to teach and learn. Such an approach encourages use of illuminating failures in the use of technology in the classroom as well as examples of best practice. Finally, these principles imply the need to build ongoing community and systems of support from peers, mentors, and experts.

## Professional Development Programmes

The International Society for Technology in Education

(ISTE) has produced a set of standards for teacher skills and knowledge in the use of technology, a useful guide for determining the content of teacher professional development programs. These standards were developed through a multiyear consultative process with thousands of teachers who were using (or trying to use) technology in their practice, principally in the United States and Canada. Another tool, the "Professional Competency Continuum," can be used to determine the skill levels of individual teachers and their professional development needs.

Policy makers should assume as a bare minimum requirement at least 24 hours (three full days) of teacher training in the use of technology. This includes basic operating systems (turning computers on and off, opening and closing files, etc.), word processing, and spreadsheets (particularly useful for such noninstructional tasks as grading). Obviously, the more time allocated for this training, particularly hands-on time, the greater the mastery of these basic skills will be. Teachers should finish this basic course with at least the fundamentals necessary for them to practice and develop their skills further back in their schools. Adding another 16 hours of training and Internet access would enable teachers to access information on the Internet, do some basic lesson planning integrating technology, and exchange e-mail messages and files with colleagues and experts. With this base of 40 hours of professional development, provided the methodology of the course incorporates some of the key interactive learning principles described above, teachers should be able to begin using technology in their classrooms.

Experience of the World Links program suggests that at least 80 hours of professional development are required before teachers can really begin to integrate technology into their teaching. Additional content would include linking curricular objectives to technology-based activities, development of lesson plans and evaluation strategies that incorporate technology, construction of educational Websites, and discussion of ethical issues related to technology and education. Ideally, this is provided in various stages, allowing time for teachers to experiment with and apply their new technological skills and knowledge in the classroom before moving on to move advanced applications. This approach also allows teachers to reflect on and share their learning experience (both positive and negative) with their peers, thereby promoting the social construction of knowledge. World Links has been a pioneer in developing and delivering teacher professional development programs in the use of technology to improve teaching and learning in developing countries. It is by no means the "definitive" program, nor is it the most easily replicated and scaled. However, for purposes of illustration, the complete World Links Teacher Professional Development program includes 200 hours of training, equivalent to five 40-hour weeks. This takes teachers with no prior contact with computers to full competency over a two- to three-year period.

In addition to content, professional development for technology should incorporate the fundamental components that research has found to be essential, including:

— *Direct connection to student learning:* The goal of teacher professional development is improved student achievement.

— *Hands-on technology use:* This requires development of

core technology competencies and skills (referred to above) and actual application of skills in the classroom.

— *Curriculum-specific applications:* To the fullest extent possible, teachers need to see a direct link between technology and the curriculum for which they are responsible.

— New roles for teachers, as facilitators and guides, not simply as lecturers or instructors.

— Active participation of teachers and collegial learning.

— Professional development as an ongoing process.

A key issue that must be addressed is teacher motivation to participate in professional development workshops in the use of technology. While so-called "champion teachers" ask for and seek out professional development opportunities in the use of technology, the vast majority of teachers do not. Teachers generally are reluctant to change their teaching styles and habits; are cautious of time-consuming activities that may take away from other high-priority obligations (economic, familial, or educational); have difficulty seeing the potential payoff beforehand of this kind of training; and may feel so threatened by technology that they want to distance themselves from it rather than embrace it. Put simply, many teachers require additional motivation and incentives to participate actively in professional development activities.

Ministries of education should be more active in designing criteria for certifying technology-focused teacher professional development programs. They can begin by seeking examples of best practices/examples of professional development programs (domestic or international), relating training programmes to existing teacher knowledge and skill standards, and comparing programs to curricula. Then, departments of inservice training should certify the best teacher training programs and link teachers' progress in salary and grade scales to successful certification. This would send a clear message to teachers and school directors that such training is valued at the highest levels of the ministry, and that it increases teachers' incentive to actively participate.

Teachers need to be encouraged by administrators, particularly their school directors, to participate in training activities. Administrators need to ensure that teachers have adequate time to participate, and do not have to sacrifice too much personal time to do so. From an administrative perspective, this should be viewed as an investment and a contribution to the capacity building of the country's teaching force. But, in addition to time allocation, supervisors should recognize publicly teachers who successfully complete professional development courses. This provides immediate personal reward to teachers, raises their status in the eyes of their peers, and encourages others to participate.

Many teachers lead an isolated professional existence, with little input from or collaboration with their peers or supervisors. Alone in front of a class of 25-75 students, they teach according to what they learned (both content and pedagogy) several or more years ago in a preservice teacher training institute. Learning new technological skills, especially if they include Internet and e-mail, allows teachers to break down the walls of their classroom and share lesson plans, evaluation strategies, student assessments, and even just the joys and frustrations of teaching.

For example, more than 80% of teachers in both Africa and Latin America who responded to the survey included in the 1999 evaluation of the World Links professional development program, conducted by SRI International, gave the highest possible ranking to the program's impact on their motivation and satisfaction as teachers. In other words, technology reduced their isolation and made them more excited about teaching. Sharing that experience should serve to motivate other teachers to participate in similar professional development programs.

Technology can speed up and increase the efficiency of a range of noninstructional teacher activities such as student attendance, grading, textbook distribution, and preparation of administrative reports. It also can enhance the productivity of basic instructional tasks, such as preparing lesson plans and class outlines, developing quizzes and examinations. More advanced applications include fast identification of educational resources (online), use of CD-ROM materials, and curriculum-linked telecollaborative programmes. In fact, there is a nearly limitless range of opportunities for teachers who develop the necessary skills and knowledge in the effective use of technology in the classroom, and who have access to technology and Internet. They can:

— plan, conduct, and evaluate learning projects with colleagues and students;

— receive and provide support following courses;

— participate in (or lead) topical discussions;

— conduct and attend course activities;

— find resources, experts, and new colleagues; and

— serve as resources for other educators.

Teachers may be motivated to participate in professional development workshops in the use of technology because they see them as an opportunity to become a trainer/ mentor for other teachers. In many cases, becoming a trainer brings additional financial and professional opportunities (travel, participation conferences, publications, etc.). If the training workshops come with some form of official certification for successful completion, motivation is enhanced further.

School directors, finance officers, and other administrative personnel also need professional development in the use of technology for noninstructional purposes. Technology can improve significantly the productivity of activities related to financial management, class scheduling, personnel management, student tracking, administrative reporting, communicating with parents, etc. However, training of school directors should not be limited to noninstructional uses of technology. It is vital that school directors understand and support teachers' efforts to integrate technology into the classroom.

Far too often, school directors minimize the time and effort required for teachers to develop the skills and knowledge required to use technology effectively, and, in many cases, directors actively oppose teachers' efforts to use technology in innovative ways. For this reason, it is strongly recommended that all school directors participate in introductory professional development workshops in the pedagogical application of technology. If at all possible, this should be done in collaboration with teachers (even students!), so school directors understand that technology requires us to be both learners and facilitators of the learning of others.

School directors need to see the potential of technology to be a catalyst for more effective learning. They also need to understand (and empathize with) the process and the time required to tap this potential. If this happens, they will be far more likely to encourage their teachers to participate in training workshops, allow them needed release time, and encourage them to experiment with innovative teaching practices using technology.

Parallel to, and in conjunction with, teacher professional development is the need to provide training for students in the use of technology. It is shared wisdom now that youth acquire technological skills far more quickly than adults, and they are far more likely to share their skills with their peers (either deliberately or simply through interaction). Rather than seeing this as a threat to their authority, teachers should embrace this reality and use it to their advantage.

Technology training for students has a "viral" character to it in that it tends to replicate itself spontaneously and spread among other students, many of whom have extremely strong intrinsic motivation to learn new skills. This motivation is related to youth's natural affinity for new technologies, their desire to improve their academic performance for downstream educational and economic opportunities, and their understanding that these skills are increasingly demanded in their countries' labor markets. Such motivation is not often present among teachers.

Technologically savvy students can help teachers use technology in the classroom in many ways, especially when collaborative, constructivist, and authentic learning strategies are used. At a basic level, students can provide technical support in the classroom to their peers and even to the teacher in the use of software, Internet research, leadership of small groups, and even simple computer maintenance and troubleshooting of common glitches. At a more advanced level, students often have more time and desire than teachers to develop their technological skills further. Thus, they can "instruct" the teachers themselves, by demonstrating new software applications, building educational Websites, and handling administration of networks/servers/IP (Internet Protocol) addresses, etc. Having students take on these responsibilities can free up time for teachers to focus on pedagogical issues, and empower them to promote a more interactive learning environment.

Generating parent support for technology in schools is important if technology investments are to be sustained and/or expanded. World Links' experience in more than 20 developing countries suggests that parents are often the primary source of recurrent financing for technology in schools and, actually, the most logical source from an economic perspective. This is because universal access to technology simply is not possible now (even if the hardware and software were free, a huge proportion of schools in developing countries lack the electricity and phone lines needed to use them), and those schools that meet basic technical criteria usually are located in more urban and/or middle-class socioeconomic areas. In other words, technology can exacerbate inequity of educational and economic opportunities within a country. With their children as the direct beneficiaries of technology-enhanced learning, parents are the natural source of financial support to sustain technology at the school level. Offering training for parents in the use of technology helps them to understand its potential for their children.

Consequently, such training makes them more likely to bear a portion of the financial burden and encourage their children to take advantage of these new opportunities. In addition, trained parents can become invaluable "monitors" or aides in school computer labs, either paid or volunteer. This eliminates the need to assign teachers to the computer lab during nonteaching hours, encourages greater school-community integration, and provides opportunities for students and adults to share their skills and knowledge with one another. In many cases, "champion students" can offer training to parents and other community members.

Once teachers have mastered the basics of ICTs-operating systems, word processing, and e-mail and Internet navigation—they can use the technology to access professional development opportunities. This enables anytime, anywhere learning and overcomes the conventional limitations of face-to-face training workshops (cost, travel, accommodations, and low numbers of participants).

## Online Professional Development

Many different technologies have been used to support or provide teacher professional development. Often grouped under the vague heading, 'distance learning,' they include basic correspondence courses, broadcast television, interactive radio, and video. The potential of new digital technologies (the Internet, digital radio, CD-ROMs, DVDs) for teacher professional development. To begin, it is important to distinguish among different approaches or models for online professional development.

Many developing countries looking to improve the quality of their preservice and/or inservice teacher professional development programs can begin here. However, this approach does not reduce costs (it increases them), nor does it replace face-to-face instructional time (the primary cost) or improve scalability of training. The online lecture model offers opportunities to reduce instructional costs and reach large numbers of teachers. It emphasizes primarily one-way delivery of high-quality content. Considerable resources often are invested in developing online instructional resources, with personal contact provided over the Internet through instructor responses to assignments and exams, moderated discussion groups.

For motivated and disciplined teachers, this model can be an effective way to provide professional development at a reasonable cost, particularly in countries where qualified teachers are in short supply. However, the loss of personal contact implied by this model typically results in extremely high dropout rates (around 50%). The online correspondence model is similar to the online lecture model, but it usually invests fewer resources in content delivery in exchange for increased personal contact with the teacher through graded assignments and examinations. Indeed, quite a few traditional correspondence training programs that used postal systems to exchange the work of participants and instructors have transferred their courses to the Internet. The cost is relatively low, but the lower quality/quantity of instruction (much of the training is actually self-paced reading) limits this model to highly motivated teachers and specialized content.

The online collaborative model emphasizes the full potential of technology to enable teacher-teacher collaboration during their training course. Typically, it emphasizes asynchronous collaboration; limited enrollment (no groups larger than 20 teachers, although these may be part of courses with much larger enrollments); and expert facilitation, trust-building activities among participants, explicit schedules, high-quality learning materials of many kinds, continuous assessment, and quality assurance with respect to instructional design, subject matter content, delivery, and impact. This model often requires more time (i.e., more money) to design and deliver than traditional face-to-face courses, but it does offer many advantages (higher impact, anytime/anywhere learning, modeling of what teachers may do in their classrooms with their students, etc.).

For developing countries, the ideal online teacher professional development program may be a hybrid of these models, combining the high-quality content delivery (lecture model) with a system of mentors/facilitators for personal feedback (correspondence model) and frequent participant collaboration on assignments/learning activities (collaborative model).

## Advantages of technology use

Over the course of 12 years, more than 15,000 teachers and administrators have been trained, using both face-to-face and distance methodologies. Teachers engage in training online on their own, at their convenience, and they can do so as often and for as long as they want. Ongoing pedagogical support and teacher networking, key ingredients of effective inservice training, are facilitated by the technology. By infusing technology into the teaching and learning process, teachers' careerlong professional development has become a continuous and planned process. Technology extends training into and beyond the classroom, no longer bound by fixed schedules or physical spaces for instruction (anytime, anywhere learning).

This potential can been seen in the evaluation of the World Links Program by SRI International, in which more than 80% of teachers surveyed reported that their attitudes about teaching improved 'a lot' or 'a great deal' as a result of their involvement in the program. The program offers access to technology and the Internet, teacher professional development, involvement in international telecollaborative projects, and development of online educational content by the teachers themselves. But perhaps more important than providing additional training opportunities, the use of the Web as the training medium exposes teachers to pedagogical practices analogous to what they may do with their own students using technology.

Teachers begin to learn skills and develop new knowledge online, through interaction with instructors, mentors, peers, and subject matter experts, modeling the potential learning experience of their students after the training. More specifically, from a pedagogical perspective, teachers working together online with their instructors, peers, and experts share and collectively construct their skills and knowledge. This replaces the traditional vertical training model of trainer imparting information 'down' to a teacher.

In the corporate world, e-learning has demonstrated over the past five years that it can cut training time by one-third, increase training effectiveness by one-third, and reduce training costs by one-third. The same efficiencies need to be explored in the public sector, even if some of the costs and technology investments are different. While experience in this area varies greatly, most observers agree that the key to successful e-learning programs. Traditional teacher training approaches simply are not equipped to deal with all of these new expectations. By contrast, ICTs can help teachers to meet these expectations, by providing productivity tools, access to information and colleagues, and collaboration opportunities.

As teachers experience these external pressures, and realize the potential of technology to help them respond, their demand for training in the use of technology will grow. Scale and complexity exacerbate the issue of teacher motivation. Ministries of education around the world are struggling for techniques and incentives to get beyond the 'champion teachers' and so-called early adopters to reach the average teacher. Paradoxically, there is both excess teacher demand for training (relative to capacity to provide it) and insufficient teacher demand for training (relative to the physical distribution of computer hardware in the schools).

New teacher professional development methodologies are required to address this issue of motivation. In the future, ministries of education will issue new standards for teacher competencies in the use of technology, which will affect both preservice and inservice teacher training levels. These standards are likely to be linked to official certification requirements and processes, so that education ministries can track the proportion of teachers who have the necessary skills and knowledge, and so that teachers have an incentive to participate. As the need and demand for teacher professional development increases, the key challenges will be ensuring content quality, reliable and appropriate training delivery infrastructure, follow-up support, and measurable outcomes—and all at an acceptable cost.

## E-learning

E-learning is a way for teachers to learn new knowledge and skills using computer network technologies. The technologies provide not just text, but also sound, video, simulations, and collaboration with other learners who may be scattered around the country or the world. Currently, most e-learning is delivered using the World Wide Web; however, future e-learning could include delivery via mobile handheld devices, cell phones, and digital video devices. The rapidly declining cost of digital video disc (DVD) production and replay offers exciting opportunities to capture the work of master teachers and trainers and share this with teachers wherever they are. Internet-enabled DVD will be available soon, so that teachers learning with a DVD will be able to access materials and resources located on the DVD itself and on the World Wide Web. A $250 DVD player linked to a computer (and perhaps an Internet connection) would bring full video and audio capabilities to professional development, in combination with community-building tools and other resources. This will open up a whole new range of visual and audio possibilities in a distance training format, which is easily scaled. As Internet access and bandwidth improve in developing countries, additional Web-based synchronous and asynchronous teacher professional development opportunities will arise.

For instance, a reliable 56 Kbps Internet connection would enable online teacher professional development that includes live voice-over-IP, file sharing, control of all participants' computer screens by the instructor-facilitator from anywhere in the world, online assessment, and many other features. The instructor-facilitator would control the microphone, be able to 'pass' it to participants when they want to ask a question or make a comment, provide individualised evaluation and support to participants, and do this with teachers located in 25 different countries simultaneously. Holding this up are basic telecommunications infrastructure, the telecommunications costs of extended online connections, and regulatory issues surrounding voice-over-IP. E-learning is rapidly developing because of four main factors:

— gradually increasing availability of higher-speed computer networks to deliver information and services;

— recognition that teachers need to 'work smarter' with constant updating of skills;

— convenient just-in-time education for teachers; and

— cost-effective alternative to traditional classroom-based education and training.

Professional development of teachers in the use and application of educational technology should be designed and implemented as part of a broader educational reform program that, at a minimum, combines technology access with teacher professional development and local content development. No strategy that ignores any of these three elements is likely to succeed beyond superficial applications. Ideally, teachers' professional development should not be isolated from other elements of instructional and noninstructional educational environments, such as curriculum reform, physical/ technological infrastructure, examinations, and research. Simply providing professional development for teachers in the use of computers and the Internet, in a situation with outdated curricula, traditional standardized test systems, and insufficient technology access, is unlikely to produce any systemic improvements in learning. In fact, the high-stakes traditional examinations system frequently operates against teachers trying to incorporate technology and encourage deeper forms of learning, which frequently are not measured by standardized tests. Success in ensuring that teachers acquire the skills and knowledge they need to use technology effectively opens the door to all kinds of new educational opportunities for both teachers and students, and downstream economic opportunities for graduating youth and their countries. It is the key to participation in the global knowledge-based economy. Accordingly, teacher professional development in the use and application of technology must be given the priority and resources it deserves, while maintaining a constructively critical eye on its costs, methodologies, and impact.

## Multimedia Development

Many nations are increasing their investments in education and education technology to support the transformation of teaching and learning. Yet, not enough attention is given to the development and availability of instructional content-ware that makes the investments in hardware economically useful and educationally meaningful. One possible reason is that equipping schools with radios, televisions, and computers and connecting them to the Internet is simple compared to developing corresponding instructional materials. For a visual artist about to create a new work, the choice of medium is a question of supreme importance. Each medium carries within it a certain relationship to the gesture, a demand for restraint, limitations of texture, hue, value, plasticity. For the educationist, the term, 'multimedia,' has become much more definite. It signals high cost, a simplistic blend of visual and aural information, and low return.

Today multimedia as a means of learning is equated with tightly structured content built by a commercial vendor—a developer. It is a product, not a possibility. The excitement of choice, of trial, of process is absent. Yet, multimedia in its broadest sense is among the most effective and egalitarian of computer-based resources available. By establishing the potential for the artful interaction between learners and content-intertwining information, skills, and even the synthesizing vision that is so important to comprehension-multimedia 'contentware' is effective across the wide range of circumstances. Multimedia can be designed to:

— enhance learning in different locations and in schools of diverse quality;

— present opportunities for students working at different rates and levels;

— provide (tirelessly, without holding up other students) repetition when repetition is warranted to reinforce skills and learning; and

— compensate, in the short term, for high student populations and limited numbers of trained and experienced teachers—in combination with robust teacher development initiatives and improvements in teachers' working conditions.

In dynamic fields, such as astrophysics, genetics, or political geography, updates to contentware can ensure that teachers and students encounter and have the chance to work with current and even cutting-edge knowledge. Such encounters tie learning to the most important events of time and underscore the general idea that knowledge itself is not fixed and finalized, that there is a universe of discoveries and a library of analyses that can be available to students. Finally, computer-based and Web-based multimedia content-ware is itself dynamic, built of bits and bytes, using software development tools that combine, in some cases, the power to create with the simplicity of use. Unlike textbooks or library-based resources, contentware has the potential to engage all stakeholders in the education system—from software developers to ministry personnel to education researchers to teachers and students-in the development of multimedia learning resources.

Multimedia as a tapestry of possibilities—for creation, experimentation, and communication—that is woven by students, teachers, researchers, and professionals, working with different tools across the range of media.

— the context for multimedia development;

— the nature and modalities of multimedia;

— the authors of multimedia resources; environments and tools for multimedia development; and

— ensuring quality in multimedia.

## Multimedia Development

A decade and more ago, national efforts to introduce ICTs in education anticipated increases in efficiency, without attending to the nature of learning and cognition, or to the distinction between skills mastered in abstraction and knowledge built to be used, expanded, and eventually transcended. To build resources that enable learners to build knowledge, broaden perspective beyond building skills and memorizing facts in the abstract; if these are educational goals, technology will prove neither cost-effective nor effective in absolute terms. If goals include enhancing analysis, synthesis, communication, and the grasping of interrelationships in the ways in which represent world, will find that technology supports and empowers all of efforts along these lines. The use of multimedia as engines of learning is conditioned by several dynamic contexts, including evolving understanding of cognitive factors with direct bearing on learning and changes in school environment ranging from infrastructure to resources to teacher development.

The emergence of technology as a change factor in education coincides with the sweeping influence of cognitive science and brain studies as a factor in the transformation of teaching and learning. The influence of both of these forces has increased with the recognition of globalization, the concomitant demonstrations of the value of innovation, and the prevalence of strong 'knowledge-work' sectors.

The Committee on Developments in the Science of Learning of the National Research Council identified five themes that changed the conceptions of learning: memory and structure of knowledge; analysis of problem solving and reasoning; early foundations; meta-cognitive processes and self-regulatory capabilities; and cultural experience and community participation. Beyond thinking skills, thinking dispositions are important-students must have sensibility to know when and how to apply their skills. Development of such competencies can be fostered by the creation of a culture of thinking in the classroom.

In this way students are able to develop successful strategies to transfer their learning to other situations. From these concepts about learning, and more recently from discussion of the skill sets needed in the 'global, knowledge economy, new pedagogical rubrics have emerged that include cooperative learning, collaborative learning, active learning, project-based learning, problem-based learning, situated learning and, most recently, learning by doing.

These approaches all aim at a transfer of emphasis away from rote-based methods and assessment, and the teacher as the 'producer' of knowledge. Instead, they emphasize the roles that analysis, synthesis, and other higher-order cognitive skills play in learning, with particular focus on learners building their own knowledge. Expanding view of multimedia must also take into account multimedia examination formats.

Students and faculty feel that incorporation of rich media in assessment can provide additional support for learning and teaching. Advances in technology, cognitive science, and measurement also show the need to reinvent large-scale assessment, and this process of reinvention may stand to benefit from incorporation of multimedia. Dynamic stimuli, such as audio, video, and animation, may make performing such tasks as problem solving more relevant to student experience. To accomplish this objective, multimedia development must consider cognitive complexity, sensitivity to instruction, meaningfulness, reliability, fairness, and linguistic appropriateness. Multimedia material produced for teaching and learning must be produced for assessment as well, with compatible goals, similar depth, and equal quality.

When developing educational multimedia resources, it is important to take into account objectives at the level of the individual learner, the school, and the state. Each has different characteristics, expectations, and needs, and the means to fulfill them are all interrelated. For this reason, development of learning resources is linked, strategically, with processes of educational reform and the transformation of teaching and learning.

They may use conceptual maps linked to Web pages that highlight different aspects of a content domain: how knowledge is acquired by experts; how problems are solved; what language is used in that domain; the current pathways of deepening knowledge; and the different possibilities of presentation for different publics of different ages. Multimedia also can broaden the scope of school learning environments by enabling experiments that otherwise would be too dangerous, too expensive, or take too long. (There are already some excellent CD-ROMs available in this niche.) And visualization and modeling tools give students the opportunity to enter into much more complex knowledge-contexts (so many of which are now necessary in world than ever before), while continuing to build their comprehension of the core knowledge of those domains.

Technology can help facilitate self-assessment and other meta-cognitive activities in students, in part by giving frequent feedback. Collaborative tools and communication tools may promote reflection and learning as a social activity, enhancing the potential for conceptual change. Interactive multimedia can play a crucial role in helping students overcome misconceptions in other ways as well. Students can be enabled to develop their hypotheses as far as possible, aided by the capabilities of well-planned multimedia.

At that extreme point of development, visual feedback can intervene, providing alternatives or deconstructing their beliefs. It is possible to produce simulations and animations that feature embedded 'expert-systems examples,' demonstrating how experts have addressed the same problems or arrived at true conclusions, only after students tried the simulations on their own.

Technology can play a crucial role in connecting schools to professionals in their communities and around the world, and by allowing the school to develop ideas and positions and make them public. What types of multimedia material support more community-centered environments? People need to see and reflect on real and very often dramatic situations. It may be useful to begin with small problem sets, in which only the most relevant variables are shown; then other variables can be inserted step by step. All of these features can be implemented in well-planned simulations. Many students are motivated to include high-quality material in their pages. With access to appropriate database of educational and multimedia resources they can search, modify, and combine such material to use in their presentations and explanations.

Clearly, there are no boundaries among these four focal areas. When construct an assessment-centered learning environment, create elements of a learner-centered environment. When build a community-centered environment, satisfy criteria for a knowledge-centered environment. Well-designed systems combine characteristics of all four.

One way to ensure the interweaving of characteristics of all such environments is to ask what resources would be required for 'hands-on, minds-on, and reality-on' learning activities.

## Nature of Multimedia

Content can be presented to learners using tools ranging from books and lectures to the Internet or even handheld computers. Each different instrument-whether a book or a handheld-communicates its content in one or more modes. A book, for example, readily accommodates text, of course, plus images that can range from line drawings to schematics to maps to photographs. These modalities and instruments offer different 'affordances' (or features that facilitate a specific type of interaction). Text, as a mode for content presentation, can present complex information, although it requires literacy, analytical, and mnemonic skills. As an instrument for text-based content presentation, books are portable and easy to read, guide sequential reading, and do not require electricity (although they do require light of some sort). They offer a balance between their ability to present large quantities of content-through both text and images—and the reader's ability to build an overview of the entire body of content-based on indexes, chapter headings, and other explicit structuring—to discover the most relevant material. A Web page, which also presents information via text and images, is easier to modify and can be linked to many other pages to provide different pathways through the text.

Of course, each instrument has its limitations as well: books are difficult to modify, and many learners find it difficult to break out of their linear pathways, and Web pages are tiring to read, require electricity and connectively, and may divert readers far from their target objectives. Each modality and instrument offers specific affordances in combination with specific limitations. In addition, factors such as design, construction, development, and support vary among specific resources of a given type. In addition, external factors, such as a region's technical infrastructure, its climate, overall education system, and even the health and nutrition of individual learners, will determine the degree to which a resource's affordances are realized and its limitations minimized.

Current major modalities for content presentation are text, images, audio, video, and simulations. Each of these modalities can be presented via many instruments. The information presented is intended to provide an overall picture of modalities and instruments only, not to enable absolute rankings. Specific designs and implementations should be analyzed relative to the objectives they are intended to support and the environments in which they will be deployed. Affordances can be optimized and limitations minimized for a given instrument in a specific implementation through appropriate design and development. In a multiplatform environment, for example, in which early- and late-model PCs are mixed with Macintosh computers, interactive simulations can be written in Java to provide multiplatform interoperability. In low-bandwidth environments, requirements for plug-ins such as Flash Player can be avoided, or CD-ROMs can be used as the primary delivery instrument.

Multimedia offers the opportunity to combine instruments and modes to radically enhance the effectiveness of learning resource development efforts. Educational publishers frequently 'bundle' CD-ROMs with textbooks, providing additional resources, updates, and other information. Interactive simulations are often 'wrapped' with text addressed directly to learners, providing contextualizing information, and with text addressed to teachers guiding them in facilitation of classroom activities, questioning strategies, and assessment. In this sense, supporting radio broadcasts or audiocassettes with print-based workbooks comprises a multimedia combination of different instruments. In all of these combinations, not only are limitations mitigated, but the strengths of each instrument are also magnified beyond the potential of any single instrument deployed in isolation. That above characteristic implies a fundamental goal of multimedia design-to combine instruments in ways that best address the requirements of a specific content domain, the abilities and deficits of targeted learners, and the infrastructure and systemic conditions of the prospective learning environment to achieve results beyond what is possible with individual instruments and isolated media.

The Internet and CD-ROMs, of course, have the potential to serve as platforms for the full range of modes-text, images, audio, video, and simulations. To this potential, the Internet adds the possibility of frequent updates, collaborative or participatory solutions, and near-infinite scalability. Bandwidth and platform constraints, however, continue to pose limits in most circumstances. In all instances, effective design and development processes are required to arrive at a creative, effective, and appropriate implementation that addresses specific parameters.

Educational gains can be maximized for every situation when the most appropriate tools are used. It is not possible, however, to give recipes for what technology tools to use or when to use them. Each case is distinct. But can try to identify situations where the use of certain instructional multimedia material regularly achieves success. In such cases, it is also important to keep in mind the infrastructure or pedagogical constraints that may impede effective use of such multimedia. Below, focus on the use of video, sound, simulation, and animation, and explore considerations that affect their development.

*Video:* Videos motivate students by showing real-life situations, in ways that are often superior to a teacher narrating them or a text describing them. Videos can be used when introducing a new theme to motivate and contextualize learning, after a topic has been addressed in a few class periods to aid students in applying the knowledge they acquired, or after an entire module is completed to show connections to other subjects and disciplines. Video production is not easy. If a video is intended for widespread use or for broadcast, required resources and resulting costs mount quickly. Professionals should be involved in production of good storyboards, lighting and shooting the video, and editing and postproduction. Beta-for-mat equipment should be used, rather than VHS, to ensure high quality. Videos produced for viewing on computers are somewhat different; resolution can be low, and it should be low for most platforms currently in schools. Such videos may be displayed to large groups via multimedia projector, or individually or in small groups on individual computer work-stations.

The Digital Video Disc (DVD) format brings benefits to schools in terms of storage and durability; however, most schools do not have DVD players, and care must be taken in all cases to ensure compatibility of disc formats and players. Short videos present a whole new arena. High-compression formats such as MPEG, RealVideo, ASF, and QuickTime are suitable for delivery over the Web or by CD-ROM, and plug-in players for these formats are available as free downloads from the Internet. Short videos can be integrated into computer activities in labs or computer-equipped classrooms. They can demonstrate dramatic effects or experiments that are too costly or dangerous to be performed in schools. Production of Web- or CD-ready videos can be accomplished through relatively low-cost processes, in labs or in the open air using a camcorder, with a robust computer workstation equipped with a video card, used for editing. Specialists are not necessary.

What could limit the wide spread of video?' Even short videos are stored as very large files, and Internet bandwidth (contingent on national infrastructure, Internet service provision, and school hardware) is a key factor for transmitting them. In addition, storage space and storage media can be problematic. Older computers, especially, may lack both hard drive space and processing power to run videos-and student workstations of all vintages generally lack hard drive space sufficient to store videos in any quantity. Complementary distribution of videos, via DVD, CD-ROMs, or VHS tapes, can address Internet- and computer-related problems. It can be effective to integrate time-sensitive information-such as news, student work, and so on-with large media resources, such as videos, distributed on fixed media.

Some multimedia authoring tools, such as Macromedia Authorware, facilitate creation of integrated online and offline media solutions.

*Sound:* Audio technology has been used widely with tape recorders and radio programs. Some uses do not depend on the production of material, but stem, instead, from good infrastructure. For instance, students can progress rapidly in language studies if they interact with students from other places; they can hear specific and authentic dialects and languages. Advanced consumer tools that support these activities include Internet Protocol Telephony, CUseeMe, and NetMeeting. In addition, the explosive popularity of various techniques for exchanging music over the Internet has already led many students to explore the power of information exchange via Web-based and peer-to-peer collaboration.

Many students are eager to produce and publish their own sound files. It is easy to channel such motivated activity toward production of materials that also have educational value-for the creator. Again, resource considerations may pose limitations: although software is not too expensive, it is necessary to have a good sound card, a good processor, and sufficient RAM (random access memory) and storage capacity. Maybe the most interesting materials that can be produced are those that explore sound and image at the same time. For example, develop an applet that explores the overlap of two sounds of equal or very close frequencies; in addition to producing the sound of both frequencies, the applet can display images of the wave superposition. Such kinds of image/sound are very effective for learning about topics that students usually find difficult. By making analogies, a teacher could guide the class through discussion and research on electrocardiography, or the differences between AM and FM transmissions. Soundry, an award-winning ThinkQuest entry, includes such an applet as well as others, like the one that shows wave fronts generated by a plane crossing the sound barrier. Other useful mixtures of sound and images might address resonance; intervals in musical tones and the analogous harmonic vibrations in nature; codification of fractals or other repeating patterns using sounds; and discussion of mini-malist changes, adaptation, and rupture. And, of course, well-designed applet-based sound-and-image combinations can benefit the study of languages.

Sound files can be kept small, and the most recent Internet browsers play all common formats. For more sophisticated formats, there are free players. Simple sound cards are not expensive. So, with reasonably current hardware, technology is not a barrier to the use of audio resources.

*Simulations* : The most remarkable aspect of simulations is interactivity, or the opportunity for the learner to change values or conditions and see what happens. This capability motivates students to formulate and test hypotheses. Simulations represent the temporal dimension visually and experientially, making them different from images, text, sound, and video. In some cases, they can enhance experiences gained in real school science labs by allowing virtual experimentation in ideal conditions. The realism of these conditions can be increased gradually. Simulations also can enable experimentation with concepts that cannot be experimented with in actual school-based labs. Such cases might call for beautiful graphics or intricate outputs. Will the simulation be used in inductions, deductions, experimentation for the testing of a hypothesis, demonstration of a complex concept, or application of knowledge the learner has already gained? Each potential role has its own parameters and requirements.

Over the course of the last decade, ICTs have reshaped the contours of production profoundly in all sectors. Changes in the development of materials for teaching and learning have occurred most visibly in an expanded range of available modalities-with interactive CD-ROMs, Web-based simulations, and intelligent tutors among the array of new resource types presented to educators and policy makers. However, the more profound shift in creation of educational resources centers on the changing identity of the authors of learning resources, and on changes in the relationship between authoring itself and learning. Before the widespread adoption of ICTs in universities and schools, educational resources were generated largely by private-sector publishers or centralized government-operated organizations. Textbooks, instructional audiotapes and videotapes, and broadcasts require substantial investment in content development, and in the capital equipment required to make that content available at scale.

University faculty and, at times, schoolteachers are engaged as subject-matter and pedagogical experts. But the production, marketing, sale, and delivery of resources to the education sector generally remains solidly under the control of a single organization-whether a ministry of education or a private vendor. For this reason, it is the organization-not the individual educators engaged by the organization-that retains ultimate control over the evolution of the learning resource. Whether the target client is seen to be a ministry-level decision maker, the head teacher of a state school, a teacher in the classroom, or the operator of a private school or tutoring business, it is most often the publisher developing a product who determines the scope of the resource, its requirements, and the kinds of learning opportunities it affords its users. In some instances, centralized developers have achieved stunning successes, especially when their efforts are focused on innovation, and when such innovation is fueled by the results of research and experience.

Institutions-universities, government- or privately funded research facilities, and international agencies-may be effective developers or sponsors of multimedia resources, initially free of cost, and market considerations that may limit development in the private sector. Successful resources or approaches may be transferred later to the private sector for support and elaboration, however. In Turkey, for example, the technology research agency, Tubitek, successfully transferred its research results in education to a start-up private-sector company, Sebit, which has released a comprehensive set of interactive test-preparation tools, with efforts underway to localize these for schools in the United States and China. Alternatively, institution-based development may provide the benefits of scaffolding experiences and innovations.

Nongovernmental and nonprofit organizations have been in the forefront in linking students in innovative and effective ways. The International Education and Resource Network began in 1988 to promote project-based collaborative learning and remains among the leaders in global, Internet-based education. With a global scope that is now approaching that of iEARN, ThinkQuest integrates knowledge-building programmes with Internet design, furthering the technical skills of national and international collaborative teams. Both the institutions and the roles they play in development of multimedia resources may vary considerably.

Private-sector activities in multimedia development can also be extremely varied. Whereas private-sector activity for much of the 1990s focused on development of CD-ROM-based multimedia, with mixed results in terms of both educational and financial success, more recent activity has explored a range of models involving the Internet. As early as 1995, a Rand Corporation study for the U.S. Department of Education linked the poor quality of CD-based education software to a fragmented and difficult-to-reach market.

Innovation has come, sporadically, when smaller companies have launched products that have focused on student creativity (e.g., HyperStudio), and when they have based development on a solid foundation of learning research.

The Cognitive Tutor math products of Carnegie Learning, Inc., exemplify an approach to multimedia development that is grounded in cognitive science, computer science, and hands—on teaching and learning. The product line addresses algebra and geometry at the secondary level in the United States. Centralized production, in this case by a private-sector developer, yields a learning resource that integrates a range of pedagogical attributes and spans an entire semesters curriculum. In this instance, a private-sector spin-off from academia has led to the development of a single, comprehensive, innovative resource. However, it is critically important to observe that this product has emerged within a competitive and mature education software market, one that places a premium on product differentiation. And within the decentralized U.S. education system, where purchasing decisions are made on a district-by-district basis, marketing costs are staggering, and the success of the product, and of the company that developed it, is far from certain.

In countries in which institutional or national organizations have not yet established education portals, private companies have rushed to fill that gap.

When private-sector development of effective CD-ROM-based educational materials has been successful, as in the case of the Cognitive Tutor, success has come despite structural factors, chiefly economic, that have tended to limit the effectiveness of resources created by centralized development. It may be instructive to review those factors historically and their effects, in part to determine their continuing effect on centralized development-for both CDs and the Internet. Chief among these factors, of course, is the persistently high cost of software development.

In the United States, private-sector development of education software remained a struggling industry throughout the 1990s, despite high levels of market and venture capitalization in the technology sector and an increasing influx of technology into the schools. By the late 1990s, high development and marketing costs and low profit margins led to the consolidation of the industry in software clearinghouses, chiefly Softkey, Broderbund, and the Learning Company. Pressures of this sort force private-sector developers to design education products for the broadest possible audience, including not only teachers and students in state schools and private schools, but also families, students using computers at home, and, in some cases, private test-preparation and tutoring companies. The nonschool segments of the developers' market base may prove to be larger and more easily reached by marketing efforts, and the decision to purchase may be made more easily. However, the various learning environments-school labs, after-school labs, and homes-provide learners with radically different circumstances.

The one-learner/one-computer configuration implied in the design of most commercially produced education software is rarely provided in a school classroom or lab. And these designs fail to support-and may actually interfere with-the essential social aspects of learning. With low profit margins and little incentive to develop 'school-only' titles, developers have little reason to assume the risks of innovation. As evidence, the

Cognitive Tutor product line was recognized in 1999 by the U.S. Department of Education as one of only five of 61 available math software products as 'exemplary'—after more than 10 years of multimedia development by the private sector.

## Teacher Developers and Collaborative Efforts

Due in part to the challenges confronting private-sector developers-and in part to changes in pedagogical approaches-teachers in many countries have been seen as partners in and even drivers of development of technology-based learning resources over the past 10 years. During the early years of multimedia development in the United States, classroom teachers drove the start-up of education software companies. New tools and new understanding of the value of the teacher's experience have combined to generate new processes to develop multimedia learning resources. Apple Computer's 1984 introduction of HyperCard gave perhaps the first promise of software learning resources developed by working teachers, and today teachers developing. Web-based resources. Three programmes initiated in the late 1990s explore teachers' potential as collaborators in resource development:

— The Educational Object Economy (EOE),

— Multimedia Educational Resource for Learning and Online Teaching (MERLOT), and

— Educational Software Objects of Tomorrow (ESCOT).

— The Educational Object Economy (EOE)

The EOE emerged out of a 1993 NSF grant to the East/West Authoring Tools Group, a coalition of universities and publishers anchored by Apple Computer's Advanced Technology Group. The initial objective of the grant was to sponsor development of menu-driven 'end-user' authoring tools that could reduce the high cost of multimedia CD-ROM development. However, the programme met with unanticipated difficulties with the repurposing of university-built tools for commercial uses. The success of subsequent efforts to enable authoring tools to generate Java output led to a crucial realization—without coordinating mechanisms, a proliferation of authors and authoring tools leads to redundant development of the 'low-hanging fruit' of software resources.

Economy launched a dynamic, database-served Website as a place where users could post interactive simulations constructed as Java applets. These small, Web-delivered simulations generally enable learners to change variables and see the results of their changes graphically and quantitatively. Lifted by waves of interest in both Java and the Internet, and in open-source development models, the EOE now features over 2,000 Java-based simulations for education. Applets have been developed and contributed freely by teachers, students, programmers, and education researchers, with meta-data that include reviews, comments, and curriculum-based activities, as well as catalog information based on an early version of the Instructional Management System (IMS) model. In roughly one-quarter of these applets, Java source code is available for modification and localization.

In particular, as the EOE collection has grown, limitations in the catalog design have become apparent, complicating resource discovery and qualification by teachers. Because the EOE repository stores only the Uniform Resource Locator (URL) for each applet, maintaining the catalog becomes significant as addresses and posting changes occur on host servers. However, since 1998, the EOE has begun shifting its focus to education systems in emerging economies, where multimedia development for education is beginning. In a three-week workshop outside of Delhi, India, teachers and students designed and developed interactive simulations targeting Indian science and math topics.

Over the past decade, many cutting-edge uses of ICTs in education have been guided by the confluence of 'active learning' and the emergence of new, easily mastered applications for multimedia development. Input devices, such as digital cameras and video camcorders, have dropped in price; video and sound editing can be accomplished on desktop computers; and Web pages and even Web animations can be built by anyone with access to a computer and the ability to read and comprehend a manual. Over the course of this same period, schools and school systems have increasingly-although in many instances not systematically-incorporated active-learning pedagogies that engage students in synthesizing information derived from research across a range of sources, and in using information as the basis for alternative presentations, ranging from original plays and musicals to literary magazines to real-world experiments in physics, chemistry, and other fields. As computing power has become available in schools, computers have been deployed as the tools of resource creation.

In some cases, active engagement in design processes has been linked with helping learners to build 'ownership' of problems, leading to knowledge creation, integration, and dissemination. In the best cases, this combination of active learning and the emergence of new, easy-to-use tools for design and development have revolved in a 'virtuous circle' of multimedia resource creation. Students, themselves, now use professional or near-professional toolsets to build conceptual understanding, express ideas, and create new resources.

To demonstrate (and build) understanding, students must organize their knowledge in rich and coherent webs. Such organization has traditionally stimulated creation of concept maps. New tools now make it possible for students to perform concept-mapping activities through the creation of hypertext webs. The latter case affords students several advantages, as they use their knowledge in authentic ways, demonstrating ownership, autonomy, and effective use of symbols, and making considerations about both the audience and context. Their constructions, then, can be considered a legitimate demonstration of understanding.

Concept mapping is a valuable form of learning, because formation of rich and coherent webs is not done instantaneously. Concept webs are built step by step, through working out new concepts and relationships. Very simple computer systems-supporting only a text editor and a browser-can support student use of hypertext and other media to develop their webs. Students can use familiar tools, such as a text editor, to write concept names and descriptions, and then save their work as HTML. After this step, they can insert navigation links (or hyperlinks) and open the text in an Internet browser accessing their computer's hard drive. When they are asked to return to this text, after completing other work on their programmes, they can then update the hyperlinks connecting both texts and start building strong and eloquent connections. Continuing this process, students link their texts to the texts of their colleagues and to their own texts produced in other disciplines; through this process, they can build their command of rich, coherent webs of understanding. In mastering this process, they also experience spontaneity in learning and the evolution of concepts. To realize the potential in HTML-based concept mapping, file management is essential.

When students who are rendering their work in hypertext learn how to insert images and animations, they become even more emotionally involved-they are proud of it and express their desire to advance to better tools to edit their 'site.' Simple visual text editors show the structure of links among arrays of pages, helping students to solidify their conceptual connections. This approach goes beyond student development of PowerPoint presentations in several ways. The simplicity of HTML-based systems allows students to work comprehensively on longer-term programmes without making files prohibitively large and difficult to manage. Also, the greater flexibility of hyperlinking in HTML affords students the ability to create intricate and organized networks that more accurately reflect their ideas and associations.

Students who designed fraction software for other students, using the Logo computer language, learned fractions better than students who were taught fractions using conventional methods. Although work along this line is promising, care must be taken because students are different. While some love to develop programs, other students with different skills may prefer to frame ideas or work on refinements. Collaborative teams can be structured to take advantage of these differences, but it is critical that, over the course of the curriculum, students have the opportunity to build skills in all areas.

## Environment for Multimedia Development

For professionals (and advanced students), many new developments in authoring tools have focused on increasing the dynamism and interactivity of Web-based resources. By consolidating several multimedia-authoring functions, enabling one or two developers to complete a resource, these tools not only cut the cost of authoring, but also enhance the potential of the Internet as a delivery pathway for contentware. Other new developments have addressed resource reuse, through compilation of search-able repositories, creation of combinable software components, and new protocol that attempt to ensure that resources-whether recombined components or integral wholes-are discoverable, modifiable, and interoperable. The longer-term implications of these protocols, such as Extensible Markup Language (XML), have yet to emerge. The overall trend, however, is toward increasing reliance on the Internet, more powerful 'on the fly' assembly and modification of content based on a learner's profile and needs, and the ability to develop contentware for implementation across many languages, platforms, and cultures.

There has been notable progress in development of professional authoring tools, allowing non-specialists to work in areas previously unavailable to them. In the past, in private-sector professional situations, a graphics designer would not engage in coding or in including his or her works in Web pages. A programmer would not incorporate a sophisticated visual design without collaborating with a graphic designer, and both might then rely on a Web designer to design a site's 'architecture,' decrease image sizes, and render pages across different platforms and browsers. Today, visual or menu-driven tools perform these functions. It is easy to import and format images, test pages on target browsers, and adjust fonts, color, and size for appropriate rendering.

There are programming tools that use time lines and preexisting scripts (behaviors) that can be inserted into an animation simply by dragging them to the objects on the screen. Visual editors contain tools to guide the producer in connecting items in databases, which is necessary to generate dynamic pages and to manage very large sites. And-just as important-software tools that earlier produced incompatible output now enable seamless interpretability and file conversion. If compare the appearance of older Web pages to new ones, see that many of the newer pages include graphical objects that move in a synchronized way. These objects describe defined trajectories, encounter other objects, or allow interactivity via mouse clicks or numerical parameters. Even pages with these elaborate effects are not, today, the work of experts or professionals. Dynamic Hypertext Markup Language (DHTML) is a standard that allows objects to move within pages. DHTML and other technologies, coupled with the latest versions of Internet browsers, include Java machines and plug-ins such as ShockWave that make creation of sophisticated animations and simulations feasible for any technically competent Web author. Macromedia's Flash, for example, with its graphical metaphor of a temporal line and movie clips, makes it possible, without writing code, to adjust objects and actions that happen on the Web pages.

Other tools, such as Photoshop, Fireworks, Dreamweaver, and GoLive, have greatly facilitated publishing and maintenance of Websites in the professional world. The expanded possibilities of this new generation of Web tools engenders situations in which one professional may assume the roles that previously might have required two or three people working in a team. Of course, the tools themselves do not substitute for the training and knowledge that a professional graphic artist, for example, brings to bear on a problem in visual design, or that a programmer uses to create a spectacularly elegant solution in code. But creative professionals and other experts are empowered to realize more complex ideas in educational multimedia than ever before, without assistance. Most simulations that appear in Web pages are created using Java, a language for programmers that has not been opened significantly to nonspecialists. However, while it is difficult to produce Java applets, it is not difficult to insert them into Web pages. And there are repositories that make these resources available and facilitate their inclusion in new Web pages, by making it possible to download the necessary files and copy only two or three lines for insertion into existing HTML pages.

The first wave of the Internet boom involved the spontaneous, enthusiastic participation of many professionals. University students and faculty seized on the new medium as a way to share ideas. The idea that anyone could have access to specialized knowledge took hold, followed by the idea that anyone-even without technical skills-could publish significant new ideas and work. The concept of 'net gain' was used to predict the exponential growth in value of networks of people and resources. Fueled by this enthusiasm, new phrases appeared describing the tremendous change that access to information and information tools would create: An 'Information Superhighway' transporting us to a 'Knowledge Economy' that would usher in an 'Information Age.' The freedom to access information and to publish has proven to be very positive. However, facing new problems: with every query, search engines overwhelm us with too many URLs. For the educator, working within the constraints of poor infrastructure and limited time, it is extremely difficult to separate relevant material from the rest.

So invented new phrases, such as 'information overload' and even 'drowning in information.' Content generators face these same difficulties and require processes to optimize production. For instance, an online course developer must combine high-quality text (written specifically for online media), images (with the trade-offs of quality and size), animations, simulations, and assessments to create an integrated, seamless experience for the learner. Weaving these different strands together is facilitated when existing material is easy to find, of course, but it is also critical for the developer to know the technical and pedagogical characteristics and the conditions of use for each component resource. With such information, developers can make decisions about acquisition, reuse, or creation. Ideally, such information, conforming to established standards, will make it possible to integrate resources built with different toolsets by different developers, or made available by different vendors.

Concerned with both aspects, excess of information and integration of resources, the education community has organized initiatives defining standard sets of meta-data, or data about data, to enable resources to be searched, evaluated, acquired, and combined. With minor differences among them, each meta-data definition contains:

— general aspects that are useful for everyone (e.g., the title and a general description);

— technical aspects that are useful for developers and integrators (e.g., the technology used, resource size, prerequisites); and

— pedagogical aspects useful for teachers, educators, and integrators (e.g., the target audience, estimated use · time, taxonomy path).

In principle, attaching meta-data to a resource ensures that the user has enough information before looking at the resource to know whether it is desirable and possible to integrate with other resources. For educational users, for example, it is critical to know if a resource is appropriate to use within a certain amount of time with students of a defined level.

Translating strings in the HTML page where a simulation is inserted is all that is necessary to reformat the simulation to run in a different language; there is no need to change the source code and then recompile the applet. To the extent possible, private-sector and institutional developers should plan for internationalization of their products. Simple processes, such as maintaining repositories of original graphics files (with their layers intact), text files, and software components, may speed translation and localization. Such preparation also will reduce the cost of subsequent updates and modifications. A remarkable advance is expected from the wide adoption of XML, which enables Web pages to be generated dynamically. In other words, when a page is requested, the server constructs it 'on the fly' from a database of elements that can include text, graphics, video and sound, and even simulations.

This new development means that one server can store and assemble elements that enable core resources-such as a video or simulation-to be embedded in Web pages in many different languages or pedagogic contexts. Popular multimedia authoring tools, such as Director and Flash, now support scripts that parse XML documents. Thus, XML and related technologies have the potential to support new architectures for internationalization of educational multimedia. To summarize, classification and preparation of multimedia for reuse in many different national and international contexts is important in a globalized world pressed by the excess of information, high development costs, and complexity of managing information and knowledge. Without adequate planning, costs in relation to benefits for translation and cataloging of multimedia resources can be very unfavorable, limiting developers' abilities to derive revenues from international markets.

If a content creator-student, teacher, or professional-identifies existing material that would be useful to include in his or her own resource, copyright issues must be addressed. Regardless of whether or not copyright notice is included, the content creator must contact the author or publisher of text, images, software code, or other resources and secure written permission to reproduce the resource. Exceptions are made for resources that explicitly state they are in the public domain. Also, in specific circumstances, resources may be reproduced for 'fair use,' whereby parts of a copyrighted work are reproduced to critique or discuss the original.

Particular attention must be paid to programmes that involve students as principal content creators. Even in the primary grades, students should be introduced to the need to cite the sources they are using, to teach them how to use other sources responsibly without plagiarizing or infringing on copyright. The ThinkQuest Internet Challenge competition is exemplary in this regard. Each year, teams of students under the guidance of a coach collaboratively develop Websites that address science, humanities, social science, and interdisciplinary subjects. The programme has been attaining extraordinary results. ThinkQuest provides resources to assist teams working with copyright, avoiding plagiarism, and citing references. For large-scale programmes that involve collaboration among many individuals and institutions, establishing procedures and policies with regard to copyright and licensing is a crucial step to ensure that all parties involved understand who will control completed resources and how available these resources will be for reproduction. When the materials are completed, licensing agreements inform end users of educational software about prohibitions against sharing, copying, or changing software code.

There are, however, licenses designed to provide incentive for further development. Open-source licensing of the Linux operating system, for example, has resulted in versions developed in more than 50 languages, a wide array of system tools and extensions, and overall improvement of the operating system as a result of contributions by thousands of programmers around the world. Open-source licenses allow code use, reuse, modification, and commercialization, with the condition that the modifications are made known and accessible-returned to the public domain—and that the derived work is also licensed as open-source. Under such conditions, many developers participate in the development, thereby establishing a large base of test users, decreasing costs of development, and increasing efficiency.

Many governments have identified strategic areas where software development should receive incentives, involving even private software development firms. Special attention must be paid to ensuring the widest possible dissemination of innovation, without barring firms from including the outcomes of development in commercially marketed products. In cases where the GPL might inhibit development by removing commercial incentives, it may be advisable to implement the Lesser General Public License (LGPL). Under the LGPL, specialized code that can be instrumental in the production of other software, such as an open library of math software, is licensed separately for use in commercial and noncommercial products. All modifications and additions to existing code must be returned to the open library, but the end product is not included in the library and can be protected under a different and a more restrictive license.

Open-source educational software is available on the Internet, much of it in the form of Java-based simulations. However, in some instances, have begun in very open modes and then have found it necessary to restrict use and access to achieve sustainability or increased control over the use of resources. The ExploreScience and ExploreMath sites are wonderful examples of the use of simulations to foster learning. In the early stages of these sites, visitors to them could download simulations onto their hard drives for use offline-a necessary feature in many schools with poor Internet access or other infrastructure limitations. New resources developed for these sites, however, can only be run over a 'live' Internet connection, although it is still possible to follow links to a classic version of the site that offers older resources in compressed, downloadable versions.

## Quality Multimedia

As the list of potential multimedia authors grows to include students, teachers, and academics, evaluation and quality assurance become critical. In specific circumstance, such as acquisition of commercial software products, any of the widely available evaluation frameworks will yield acceptable results, including:

— California Information Technology Clearinghouse (CITC)

— American Dental Association (ADA) Guidelines for the design of educational software

Of these and others that are used widely, the ADA framework is surprisingly comprehensive and easily applied. Its major categories include:

— pedagogical issues (e.g., instructional methodology),

— subject matter (e.g., information accuracy),

— language and format (e.g., appropriateness, presentation),

— surface features (e.g., interface design),

— questions (e.g., assessment),

— feedback (e.g., meta-cognitive support),

— invisible functions (e.g., record keeping, security), and

— formative evaluation (e.g., testing and evaluation during development).

It is important in applying any framework of evaluation, however, to bear in mind strategic educational objectives as well as the overall context of software support for education. It is equally important to be prepared to recognize the strokes of creativity and innovation that may fall outside the range of existing frameworks, but that distinguish excellence from the norm. However, broaden understanding of authoring to include the contributions of teachers and students, the parameters of evaluation shift. When students are engaged in design-related activities, for example, strategic goals may include maximizing participation in both creating and evaluating multimedia, in addition to factual accuracy, clarity of presentation, and effectiveness. When teachers and university faculty, taking advantage of the powerful new tools at their disposal, assume the role of designers or developers, software evaluation and quality assurance again must be approached with a degree of creativity. The effort to build participation in multimedia development throughout the educational community may require incentives-such as those provided by peer review-and safeguards of field templates, testing, and other measures.

For professional and institutional developers working in resource—rich environments and under great pressures to succeed, evaluating materials after they are completed may be too late. Critical resources, including time and money, will have been expended. While functionality testing may ensure that the product works in its intended environment, it will fail to reveal flaws in the instructional design and perhaps in the design of the interface. Even review by panels of experts may not uncover the fact that the target audiencesay, upper elementary students-finds the visual design dated, the interface too complex, and the rewards for success not motivating. The product may work flawlessly as designed, but it may fail to work with learners. Iterative usability testing should be woven throughout product design and development, as a means of ensuring that these processes are meeting their overall goals, not only their programmes milestones. Testing may involve observation of users working with the product, and questionnaires, even review of individual navigation histories on a given Website. Subject-matter experts, designers, and engineers may not be familiar with current practice in this arena, and may feel initially that such measures impede their progress. However, working with trained personnel, they can quickly recognize the clear and significant benefits of integrating usability testing into resource development.

Multimedia resources-considered in terms of both products and processes—have great potential to enhance education. New modalities and instruments for development and delivery have radically increased the support that these resources can give students across a wide range of learning activities. Despite the glamour of technology-rich environments, focus must remain on learners and their motivations and challenges, on the knowledge domains to be explored, and on the communities in which learning will take place. Teachers, and students all have roles to play in the creation of multimedia, and one of the chief goals of policy must be to support appropriate activities by each of these groups. Flexibility is a key property of multimedia contentware, and must be marshaled effectively in development efforts. Despite the complexity of their interaction, the contexts for development and implementation-cognitive, instructional, and technological—can be balanced so as to advance strategic goals and plans within education systems. Cognitive science, in particular, can guide and give shape to innovation in the development of learning environments, multimedia resources, and teaching and learning practice. Both institutional and private-sector developers can draw on advances in learning science to design innovative and effective contentware.

The trends in authoring tools and pedagogy support the active engagement of students as designers, as creators, and as publishers. The LabVirt project, ThinkQuest, and iEARN engage students in collaborative problem solving through design-based activities. However, students are strongly motivated by the many new media possibilities for information exchange and communication, such as MP3 files, instant messaging, and peer-to-peer networking. These and other media should be kept in mind, and integrated into ICT planning when the opportunity arises. Authoring tools support increased ease-of-use and increased power, creating change in development teams and processes at all levels, from the professional to the student. These tools also give rise to new economies, based on reuse, shared code, and more flexible platforms. Institutional and professional developers can create resources that are compatible with the computing platforms and communications infrastructures available to their target populations.

Development at all levels-by students, teachers, and professionals-can be promoted through the establishment of libraries or repositories of multimedia resources. Such repositories become focal points for active collaboration, sharing of information, and reuse of material. Appropriate protection of intellectual property and of public access must be balanced, using mechanisms that may include the LGPL or the GPL. As always, factors outside the development processes and even outside the educational systems affect the creation of effective resources. It is vital for policy makers to influence funding, licensing, and standards for the development of educational multimedia by the private sector. Leading-edge technologies, including tools for adaptive and collaborative learning, will be introduced only with appropriate guidance and effective incentives, yet such tools are vital to realizing the promise that technology holds for personalized instruction and for the integration of higher-order thinking into all aspects of education.

## Development of the Technology Plan

The development of the technology plan involves three phases, including:

— *Organizational Phase*: The Technology Planning Team is formed with representatives from key stakeholder groups. The scope of work is determined and the planning tasks to be accomplished are identified.

— *Assessment and Analysis Phase*: An analysis is made of the present situation including the present level of technology knowledge and skills of teacher educators, the teacher education curriculum and performance results, national teacher technology standards, condition of teacher education facilities, and the current technology resources and infrastructure within teacher education programmes or institutions. A powerful vision for ICTs in teacher education is developed focused on improving teaching and learning. Specific goals and objectives are developed to achieve the vision.

— *Formulation Phase*: Based on the vision, goals and objectives, a technology plan is developed including standards and models for technology and learning, hardware and software requirements, staff development plans, technology support services to be provided, facility improvement requirements, project timelines, areas of responsibility, and a detailed budget. These items are integrated into a comprehensive technology plan that is submitted for review and approval.

The organizational phase of the development of the technology plan involves the following activities: selecting the team leader, forming the planning team, determining the scope of the planning effort, and identifying the budget and time constraints for completion of the plan.

It is important to select a qualified person to lead the planning effort. The person should be chosen by the chief executive of the institution or government organization responsible for the development of the plan. The person selected should have the commitment and support of the organization's highest administrators, and have high credibility in the organization as well as with teacher educators and other important stakeholder groups.

The person selected need not be a technology expert, but should be someone who understands the potential of technology to improve education and has the communication, management, and interpersonal skills to lead the team and communicate with stakeholder groups in developing the plan.

The members of the team should be chosen carefully because it is important to establish a team that has the commitment, leadership, and needed expertise in teacher education, ICTs, and K-12 education. The planning team should be composed of individuals from the teacher education institution or agency developing the plan and representatives from external stakeholder groups.

The team should include teacher educators, administrators, pre-service and in-service teachers, and members of other key stakeholder groups who will be affected by the plan. If the plan is developed within an institution of higher education, it is also important to have representation on the team from university computing services and other units in the institution that offer courses taken by students in the teacher education programme. The team should also include members who can contribute resources or expertise to the plan or whose support will be critical to the plan's acceptance.

Ultimately the commitment, expertise, and perspectives of the planning team members will determine the quality of the plan. It is often helpful for members to engage in team-building activities to get to know each other and become familiar with the rich range of expertise and diverse perspectives that exist within the team.

As a first task, the team must understand the scope of work, timelines, and budget constraints for developing the technology plan.

It is critical to understand the deadline for completion of the plan and to set milestones and timelines for completing each component of the plan. Planning always takes longer than expected, because a critical and time-consuming aspect of the planning process is building consensus on critical elements among the team members and stakeholder groups. It will not be possible to achieve consensus on every aspect of the plan, and at times the planning team or planning leader may need to make final decisions on specific plan elements.

The second major phase of the planning process is the Assessment and Analysis Phase. In this phase: the team will determine the present status of ICTs in the teacher education programme or institution that is the focus of the planning effort. This involves assessing the status of ICTs in teacher education and developing a powerful vision of learning with technology.

The planning effort may be thought of as a journey or a quest. Before setting out on this quest, it is necessary to know the state of ICTs in teacher education at present. The vision describes the destination or desired state of ICTs in teacher education in the team's country, region, or institution. The plan serves as the 'road map ' to help the programme move from the current state to the desired state.

In order to understand the teacher education programme's current situation in relation to the national or international continuum, it is helpful to look at current issues and trends in the integration of ICTs into teacher education at the national and international level.

## Assessment Tools for Teacher Education

The 'New Economy, whether described as the information economy, digital economy, or knowledge economy, has produced significant changes in agriculture, industry, business and many other aspects of global society. It is also beginning to change our educational institutions and the teaching-learning process. It is important to understand what it takes for technology to improve learning. In developing the plan, consider the following conditions that are essential for schools to derive the full benefits of the new tools for learning:

Teacher educators, teachers, and students have meaningful access to technology. Internet and communication capabilities are available to access libraries, museums, locally, nationally, and around the world.

Understanding current issues and trends in learning theory will provide the planning team helpful information for developing its vision of ICTs in teacher education. It is important early in the planning process to determine the level of accessibility of ICTs in the teacher education programme and the extent to which technology is integrated into the curriculum and instructional practices of teacher educators.

The Tech teacher education programmes have limited technology resources and infrastructure. Most of the available technology resources are 5+years old. The programme receives less funding than other campus programmes. There is limited partnership with schools for technology. There is limited technical support and less than 25% of the methods and content courses integrate technology into the curriculum.

Most teacher educators are at an early adoption stage in using technology and have had little or no technology training. Developing Tech teacher education programmes have some clear goals and the level of funding for technology equals that of most higher education programmes. Technology is integrated into 50% of the courses and in the field experiences of students. Funding is about the same as other programmes on campus and there are growing investments in technology. The equipment is 3-5 years old.

The teacher education faculties are either at the adoption or adaptation level in using technology with 75% using technology in their teaching practices. The institution rewards expertise in using technology in teaching and research. In addition, technology training workshops and technical support are provided to the teacher educators. Advanced Tech teacher preparation programmes are focused on continuous improvement of the programme.

Funding for technology equals the top 2 -3 programmes on campus and technology is integrated into most of the courses and into 75% of the field experiences. The teacher educators are at the adaptation or appropriation level in understanding and use of technology to enhance learning. Target Tech teacher education programmes integrate technology throughout the curriculum and into all teaching practices. Students and teacher educators use current digital resources both in the classroom and online.

Pre-service and in-service teachers and teacher educators use digital means to communicate with each other and with experts locally, nationally, and globally. All graduates meet the highest standards of technology teaching expertise, are sought after for these skills, and become technology leaders in their schools.

In planning to integrate ICTs into teacher education, it is important for teacher education institutions to understand types and levels of knowledge and skills needed for teachers to effectively use ICTs in instruction. They must also understand the level of readiness of the institution to integrate technology into the teacher education curriculum.

The teacher education programme or institution must know the benchmarks, standards and guidelines for ICTs in teacher education. It is also important that they have access to tools that help the institution assess its level of readiness or progress toward infusing ICTs into the teacher education programme.

A number of tools may be used as developed, or adapted as needed, to help the technology planning team assess the level of technology integration in their teacher education programme prior to developing plans for integrating ICTs into the curriculum.

There were number of web-based tools available to help the planning team or teacher education institutions assess their progress in incorporating ICTs into teacher education. Some of these tools are specifically for teacher education programmes and higher education institutions while others are designed for assessing technology integration or level of readiness for technology in K-12 schools. The K-12 profile or survey instruments have often been used or customized to yield information that is useful for assessing the status of technology infusion in teacher education.

Several of the assessment tools are web-based and allow for online form submission and the automatic analysis of responses. Teacher educators may use some of the tools to provide a profile for self-assessment of technology use, knowledge, and skills.

Other tools are designed to provide a profile for an entire school, college, or teacher preparation programme and may serve as useful indicators of the present level of readiness for the integration of technology into the programme. Many of the forms may also be used in a paper-pencil mode if desired. Although designed for K-12 schools, the tools can be used by teacher preparation institutions to develop a comprehensive technology plan.

Technology Integration in Teacher Preparation is a tool developed at the Technology Leadership Academy at the University of Texas at Austin to assist teacher preparation programmes in monitoring progress toward technology integration. It provides descriptive indicators for each target.

To use Targets for Technology Integration as an institutional self-assessment tool, one or more members of the faculty or administration complete the survey indicating their best estimate of their institution's status in each of the target components.

Learning With Technology Profile Tool helps teachers compare their current instructional practices with a set of indicators for engaged learning and high-performance technology. The tool was developed by the North Central Regional Educational Laboratory for use by K-12 teachers but may also be used,or adapted for use, with teacher educators to help them assess their current instructional practices.

The PCC online assessment tool was developed primarily for K-12 teachers but is potentially useful for teacher educators. Developed by The Milken Exchange on Educational Technology, the tool provides educators with an opportunity to assess their status within the skill and knowledge areas described in that continuum.

Developed and distributed by The Teaching, Learning, and Technology Group (TLT), the tool helps faculty participants design customized web-based questionnaires from hundreds of self-rating and open-ended questions on student back-ground, use, experience with technology, and satisfaction with course experiences.

Use of the above assessment tools can help teacher education institutions assess their present status and levels of readiness to integrate technology into the teacher education curriculum. These tools can also help the planning team establish benchmarks and monitor the progress of the implementation of the plan.

The goal of technology infusion in schools is to improve student learning. One of the first tasks in the development of a technology plan is to identify the strengths and weaknesses of current teacher education programmes.

One way to determine teacher education programme performance results is to examine the data from exit assessments, certification tests used for graduating teachers, or other relevant data. It is important to determine the knowledge and expertise of teacher education students in using technology in instruction. This may be done in various ways such as by observing pre-serv-ice or in-service teachers using technology in instruction, by examining electronic portfolios of students ' academic work, or by examining technology competency evaluations by supervising or mentor teachers.

For example, an international study of eighth grade mathematics showed that middle school students using open-ended, problem-solving software significantly improved mathematics performance. Similarly, a number of technology tools and programs can help improve learning in science. Research also shows that technology can help improve writing, the learning of social sciences, foreign languages, and other elements of the curriculum. In examining student performance data, it is important to assess the technology knowledge and expertise of graduating teachers in using technology in instruction. One way to do this is to ask pre-service teachers to compile an electronic portfolio of their work that demonstrates specific technology competencies.

To determine a school's technology resources it is important for the team to review or develop a complete inventory of the existing hardware and software within the teacher education institution. Existing inventories may be used for this purpose or the institution's inventory control or technical staff may prepare summaries of the types and quantities of hardware and software used in teacher education. In looking at the hardware inventory summary data, the planning team must determine not only the level of access to technology by teacher educators and students, but also the age and capabilities of the technology.

For example, older computers may not have sufficient capabilities to access Internet resources. New facilities can be built in ways that reduce the cost of technology adoption later on; for example, incorporating appropriate wiring or at least wiring ducts in new buildings greatly reduces the cost of adding technology later. The Higher Education Information Resources Alliance has developed a set of guidelines that colleges and universities can use when conducting institutional self-assessments of their technology facilities and resources.

The assessment of teacher educator technology competencies should be based on the national, provincial or state standards for teacher technology knowledge and skills. The standards are efforts to identify the core knowledge and skills necessary for teachers to effectively use ICTs to enhance learning. If standards for teacher technology competency do not presently exist, it is helpful to look at standards for student knowledge and skill in using technology.

These standards may be helpful in considering the core technology competencies also needed by teachers. It may also be helpful to view teacher technology standards used by other countries. The NETS have been used in the United States and have been adopted or adapted by a number of other countries to meet the needs of their educational systems.

In establishing a baseline for the technology plan, it is important to understand the present levels of technology proficiency of teacher educators in the teacher education programme. Other means of assessing the present levels of integration of technology into the pre-serv-ice programme may include interviewing teacher educators on their use of tech-nology,reviewing course syllabi for evidence of technology use in the course, and observing the level and type of technology use in the programme classes.

Based on the assessment of the present levels of teacher educator knowledge and skill in using technology, the planning team can better determine the professional development needed to help the teacher educators develop the desired competencies. It is also important to determine the present levels of technical support provided to teacher education faculty and to identify the level and types of support needed to facilitate increased and effective use of technology in instruction.

In developing the technology plan, it is important to keep stakeholders informed throughout the entire planning process by sharing information on the current situation of ICTs in teacher education, the identified needs, and the vision, mission, and objectives of the plan. It is also important to get input from all stakeholders to help build support and advocacy for the technology plan.

Many impressive technology plans have failed because of the lack of effective communication with key stakeholder groups. Consequently, a critical element for the success of a planning effort is to develop an effective communication strategy. Such a strategy will:

— enhance consensus-building efforts by keeping everyone informed;

— attract potential business and community partners to the university or school;

— help attract in-kind contributions in support of the plan.

In a very real sense, the members of the planning team must also become effective communicators to stakeholder groups. As the team progresses through the planning process, they should meet with key stakeholder groups and determine the potential strengths and barriers to the plan's implementation. The emerging plan may then be modified to address concerns or obstacles, and the team can tell stakeholders how these concerns will be addressed.

The communication strategy may involve meeting with university administration, faculty, students, K-12 school administrators and teachers, national, state, or provincial educational agencies, business leaders, and community, civic or international organizations.

The results of the assessment should be summarized in a form that is easy for others to understand and should establish a clear picture of the present state of ICTs in the teacher education programme.

## Vision of ICTs in Teacher Education

Knowing the current situation of ICTs in teacher education, the next step is to develop the vision statement that will serve as the focus of the strategic technology plan. A vision statement is the grand, global statement around which a teacher education institution will be focused for action.

It is the most important part of the strategic technology plan and will guide the development of all of the elements of the plan. It describes a set of ideal circumstances that the teacher education programme will strive to achieve. The vision statement should provide:

— a clear and concise statement of the team's vision for using technology to improve learning and teacher education;

— an indication of who will use the technology and how it will be used to enhance learning;

— an indication of the envisioned benefits that will result from the use of technology by pre-service or in-service teachers, teacher educators, administrators and others.

The plan's goals, objectives, and implementation activities must tie back into the vision statement. The vision statement should be used to check the validity of any goal or activity specified in the strategic plan. For example, if the plan specifies the creation of interactive distance learning classrooms in the teacher education institution, the reason for creating those classrooms should be implicit in the vision statement.

The vision statement of the technology plan should be focused on learning and provide a clear idea of how the vision will help prepare a new generation of teachers who are able to effectively use the new and powerful ICT tools for learning. There are two approaches for developing a vision. In one approach, the vision is developed prior to identifying the teacher education programme's status in integrating technology into the learning process.

The advantage of this approach is that it often leads to creative visions that are not constrained by the realities of the current resources and context. The other approach involves developing the vision after a careful assessment of the status. The advantage of this approach is that it may result in a more "doable" vision.

Strategic planning is combining what is known today with lessons learned from the past to develop a plan to set and accomplish the vision, mission, goals, and action plans of the teacher education programme.

Visioning is about conceiving a desired future state, a picture of where and what the teacher education programme should be in the future, without being constrained by such factors as funding or resources, and then working backward to develop an action plan to get there. It is about imagination and discovery, not simply analysis and forecasts.

Vision represents the following characteristics:

— *Visions are grand and exciting*: Visions inspire and challenge the organization and its members. They capture the imagination. Little visions are not worth committing years to create, but a grand vision is something everyone can understand intuitively, take pride in, and work towards. Such visions can be the single most powerful influence on an organization's destination. Successful technology plans are driven by vision; they are not driven by a chain of command.

— *Visions focus on the end state:* Visions can act like internal gyroscopes, directing individuals and their schools, building positive expectations for success, and reducing fear of failure. A visionary teacher education institution or school knows what its future looks like; therefore, it can better recognize and seize opportunities that lead to it.

— *Visions are holistic*: Visions are holographic and they happen at multiple levels within the teacher education programme-personal, departmental, institutional, even community wide. Individuals see an image of themselves in the vision, what they would like to become, or how they would like to meet future challenges.

Stakeholders also need to be part of the visioning process because it is important that the vision statement represent an invitation to own the future together. A process that empowers many people through shared dialogue and teamwork adds great value to strategic planning. The learning community can enlarge its circle of influence through this process.

Goals are broad, comprehensive statements that identify the intended outcomes of the technology plan. They are statements of how the vision and mission statements will be achieved. The goals should specify the accomplishments needed if the vision is to become a reality, and should be clear, realistic, and attainable. The objectives are delineated from the goals and make clear how they will be achieved. They represent the specific steps-the specific activities-that must be accomplished to achieve each goal.

The final phase in developing a technology plan is the formulation phase. In this phase the planning team develops the detailed plans for the teacher education institution to achieve the vision, mission, goals, and objectives of the plan. The team identifies specific projects, timelines for completing each component of the plan, and budgets.

The stakeholders, including those responsible for carrying out the technology plan, must understand what is needed and what must be done to accomplish the vision. The plan must show how the technology will support the curriculum and enhance meaningful, engaged learning for those in the teacher education programme.

A well-written technology plan will answer clearly the who, what, when, where, why, and how questions related to achieving the vision and goals. The many tasks involved in creating the technology plan will require a division of work among members of the planning team.

The process may also require the support and participation of staff or consultants with needed expertise. This resource provides a number of web-based instruments that can be used to acquire and analyze information needed to develop the plan. The free resource provides a database of the information collected and analyzed in the technology plan.

One of the most important tasks in developing the technology plan is to determine the specific technology needed to achieve its vision and goals. The technology standards and requirements component of the plan will identify the hardware and connectivity/infrastructure standards to support the planned learning environments. It will also identify general software requirements and provide examples of the software needed to address the learning goals and objectives.

To develop the standards and requirements, the planning team must first understand the current resources available to the teacher education programme and then identify the additional requirements needed to meet the goals and objectives of the plan. In some instances, teacher education institutions and schools identify their hardware and network software requirements before they choose the software to support the curriculum and teaching-learning process.

In developing the software standards and requirements, it is important to first review the software inventory information to identify what software is currently available and what will be needed to support the plan. Although the plan might not list all the software programs that are related to the objectives, it may give examples of the types of software programs congruent with the vision of the learning process and the school curriculum. In developing the software requirements, the following types of software programs may be considered:

— *Tool software*: These are generic tools that may be used across content areas and include word processing, spreadsheets, databases, desktop publishing, multimedia, presentation, and web development.

— *Curriculum-focused software*: These include software programs with content or functions designed to address a component of a specific educational discipline or knowledge domain (e.g., learning specific mathematical or science concepts).

In identifying software needs, it is important to recognize that the quality of educational software varies greatly and thus software must be chosen carefully to best meet the programme's needs. In some contexts, there may be a lack of high quality, culturally responsive software. The plan may include provisions for the development of software to meet specific needs of the teacher preparation programme or the national educational system.

Teacher educators working with pre-service and in-service teachers and technology and media experts may develop software to address critical needs. The next step in the planning process is to identify the technology equipment and learning devices that will be needed to meet the instructional objectives of the teacher education programme.

Standards and requirements for the hardware need to be identified. At one time, the term hardware referred only to computers; however, now it refers to an endless list of computers, peripherals, presentation tools, and broadcasting and networking equipment. The numbers and types of computers and other equipment needed will depend on the plan's vision of how technology may enhance learning.

Computers labs provide a convenient means for access to technology for a large number of users. They concentrate expensive resources in a single location that can be used by entire classes during instruction or as an open laboratory for individual student use at other times of the day. They reduce the costs of installing electricity, networking infrastructure, and servers to support use of the computers, and allow for more effective security. They also reduce connectivity costs to the Internet. The room selected may be larger than conventional classrooms to provide space for students to work collaboratively.

The computer lab option also produces a number of constraints, such as competition among teacher education classes for access to the lab. Scheduling individual class use of the facility can be complex and may frustrate teacher educators and inhibit their use of the technology. It also makes just-in-time use of the technology by classes for learning projects and activities more difficult.

Placing computers in libraries is an effective approach in situations where only a few computers may be acquired. This allows all students and teacher educators to have access to the computers, and to use staff available to provide assistance in accessing relevant information resources on the Internet. Computers may be placed in common rooms where instructors may use the technology for accessing relevant information and learning resources or to develop lesson plans.

Multimedia carts ,comprised of a computer, projector, and VCR allow instructors to demonstrate instructional uses of technology in their classrooms. If wireless access to the Internet is available in the building, the computer cart may be equipped with a wireless network card so that the instructor can access or demonstrate learning resources available on the Web. Providing computers in individual classrooms makes it possible for the technology to be accessed and used as part of the ongoing instructional process.

However, it requires more than a few computers to be placed in the classroom, otherwise it will be difficult for the teacher educator to integrate the technology into the teaching-learning process. Placing computers in individual classrooms also provides a number of challenges such as the cost of providing electricity and connectivity to each room, renovation costs, space constraints, and costs for software and supplies to be used. It also poses challenges in providing security, maintenance and support services for the distributed computers.

A mobile computer lab consists of a mobile cart containing a printer, wireless access point, and a classroom set of 20-25 laptop computers equipped with batteries and wireless network cards. The computers may be moved from classroom to classroom and shared by teacher educators. The mobile computer lab reduces the costs for installing electricity and connectivity in the classrooms.

The laptop computers do not require special furniture and can be used by students at their desks. Printing can be done via the wireless network. The mobile lab also provides the benefit of lower software costs, similar to that provided by a computer lab. In addition, the mobile carts can be stored in a secure area when not in classroom use. The mobile computer lab does pose some problematic issues that must be considered.

The laptop computers are typically more costly than desktop computers, and the mobile computer lab provides the same potential for scheduling conflicts as noted for the computer labs. The mobile lab cannot be moved between the floors of a building without elevators and is difficult to move between buildings unless there is a smooth walkway connecting the buildings.

The use of the mobile lab requires a system for delivering the cart before each classroom use and retrieving the cart after the class, and instructors need to be trained in these procedures. In developing the hardware requirements section of the plan, it is not necessary to specify the specific models of computers to be acquired

One of the most critical elements of the technology system is the infrastructure that supports the network and provides the connectivity and communication capabilities for each of the connected computers. Planning the network infrastructure is an essential element of the technology planning process and the plan should be designed to meet not only the current needs, but also have sufficient capacity to meet future requirements.

The goal should be to establish information systems and infrastructure which maximize connections among teacher educators, pre-service and in-service teachers, and students, and which provide access to expertise and information resources from universities, museums, libraries, and databases around the world.

The most significant factor in enabling teacher educators to integrate technology into the instructional process is faculty development. Too often technology plans provide substantial funding for the acquisition of hardware and infrastructure but provide limited funding for the needed professional development and support.

Successful programmes for training teacher educators to integrate technology are emerging after years of experimentation. Three essential factors related to creating a successful teacher educator professional development programme are:

— First, administrators must provide development programmes that serve teacher educators with very different skills, needs, and interests. A fully rounded training programme should include not only introductory classes for those who need to learn the basics, but more advanced classes as well. It should have in-session training seminars and online courses. It should have short, targeted programmes that tackle one subject in a couple of hours (how to create a Power Point presentation, for example) as well as semester-long courses or workshops.

— Second, effective development programmes involve teacher educators at every stage of the process. Teacher educators must identify their training needs, help plan the curricula, act as mentors, and provide feedback. In addition, teacher educators must be committed to using their newly developed skills in the classroom as soon as possible, because the training lessons will fade over time.

— Third, the best programmes use technology to teach technology. This type of hands-on exposure greatly enhances the acquisition of necessary skills. Engage the teacher educators in projects during training classes and in follow-up activities at their institutions or schools in order to cement the lessons learned.

The technology plan needs to identify the services needed to support the implementation of the plan. Providing the equipment, software, and training will launch the programme, but for it to be successful, it must provide for the ongoing and long-term support of technology systems. Failure to provide for support will lead to a gradual decline and eventual rejection of the new technologies that have been so carefully planned to improve learning. Technical support is needed to maintain the network, servers, and computers in the computer laboratories, classrooms, and staff offices.

In developing the technology support system, institutions will often hire a network administrator or technician because of their specialized skills; yet also expect this person to assist the teachers in the application of technology in instruction. This typically does not work well, because the technology specialist lacks the pedagogical knowledge needed to help teachers in technology integration.

## Integration of ICT and Teacher Education

The most critical factor in the successful integration of ICTs into teacher education is the extent to which the teacher educators have the knowledge and skills for modelling the use of ICTs in their own teaching practices. To enable them to develop these skills requires a well-conceived and sustained programme of professional development.

Countries that have initiated efforts to infuse ICTs into teacher education have found four professional development strategies helpful in successful technology integration.

First, professional development needs to focus on teaching and learning rather than on hardware and software. It should be designed by first considering what student teachers are expected to know and be able to do in a specific discipline, and then infusing ICTs into the learning process so that acquiring the knowledge and skills is more efficient.

Second, professional development is practically useless unless leaders and teacher educators are provided with access to technology resources and have the time and support-when needed - to apply the new knowledge and skills that they have learned. A just-in-time approach to professional development is a model that works well. In this approach, professional development is provided to teacher educators when they have a need or opportunity to use a specific technology tool or application to enhance learning.

Third, professional development in the use of ICTs is not a one-time activity. To keep current with new developments means that professional development in ICTs must be an ongoing process.

A further strategy for professional development is to start in a small way. Start by providing professional development in the use of ICTs to a small group of teaching staff. Perhaps this group will have volunteered or demonstrated that they have basic ICT competencies for personal use, or have expressed personal interest in using ICTs in their teaching. Working with this small group allows the professional development staff to determine the specific interests and needs of the teacher educators and what works best in the professional development process.

Professional development may be provided to other small groups of faculty, thus expanding and refining the professional development efforts. The most important criterion for effective professional development is to tailor it to the learning needs and skill levels of individual teaching staff within a faculty. This suggests that, ideally, an institution should, based on availability of resources, provide a variety of options for professional development for the faculty.

In structuring professional development options and resources, it is helpful to explore collaboration opportunities with partners outside the university. The opportunities for ICTs to create new paradigms of teaching and learning will depend largely on leadership and a shared vision, and on appropriate and continuing professional development.

The planning and implementation of ICT-related professional development of teacher educators should be led by a planning group that includes representation and expertise from teacher educators, programme administrators, teachers, school administrators, technology experts, and business leaders.

The diverse perspectives of the group should provide an understanding of the realities of the classroom, new views of the teaching-learning process, knowledge of the array of technologies that may be used to enhance learning, and community opinions. It is important for a planning group to negotiate a shared understanding of the role of ICTs in the agenda for educational renewal based on their individual cares and concerns.

It is also helpful to have a larger advisory or liaison group that may facilitate collaborative professional development efforts and sharing of resources across related organizations, for example, between the university and the partner schools where students are placed for teaching practice. An important aspect of professional development is not only enabling teacher educators to understand and use ICT tools in their teaching practices, but understanding how technology coupled with new approaches to teaching and learning, may enhance student learning.

Many teacher educators recognize that approaches to education are changing and that new technology has the potential to improve education and student learning. They may also recognize the implications of increasing use of technology in society and employment, including employment directly related to their own disciplines and content areas. Less obvious are the implications for literacy and numeracy at the core of the educational process, and the need for teacher educators themselves to model good practice in their teaching so that their students can easily transfer these strategies into their own teaching practice.

Teacher educators are experts in a domain, and it is important to respect this domain while helping them to revitalize and modernize their teaching with ICTs. Similarly, the risk that established teacher educators must take to develop their practice needs to be recognized and mitigated as much as possible.

The most significant change required of individuals and organizations providing teacher education is to redefine student roles and responsibilities. Both students and teachers have always had rights and responsibilities, but the redefinition of the learning environment requires a change in the balance of rights and responsibilities, with the student assuming more of both.

ICTs demand this shift because technologies are constantly changing. Students need to develop the ability to think for themselves, continually learn as technologies change, and provide support to one another. This last element, peer teaching, is a natural product of ICTs because often the younger generations bring increasingly high levels of competence into the learning environment. This is a positive shift, and it should be noted that these strategies are also appropriate for competencies that do not involve ICTs.

## Professional Development Stages for ICT

Teachers and teacher educators develop ICT competence in stages. Those who are fluent with technology may not appreciate how difficult it is for technology novices to appropriate ICTs into their professional practice. Teacher educators often find this task even more difficult than teachers do, because they typically have higher levels of content and pedagogical expertise that must be respected.

Teacher educators, because they have to work in multiple contexts-both the home institution and the field where students are placed to observe and practice teaching-may also be more influenced by the absence of the essential conditions for ICTs in teacher education.

Four stages are common, but they may be repeated with new forms of ICTs or applications of ICTs to new areas. The first stage for each individual is awareness, and the appropriate response at this stage is to provide information about a relevant application of ICTs and appropriate ways that it may be used in the individual's current professional or personal concerns.

Teacher educators then explore the use of the application. They need support to put this ICT application into practice in a timely manner and to reflect on its effectiveness. Only after teacher educators have gone through these stages are they able to adapt their practice to make better use of ICTs, and then move toward the final stage to become innovators and modellers of excellent practice for their students and colleagues.

The advent of ICTs provides the opportunity to engage in this process from a new perspective and to model processes of learning for colleagues and students. It is acceptable for teacher educators to adopt only those aspects of ICTs that are relevant to their practice, but they must first be allowed to explore the range of possibilities, so that they and their students may become critically aware of, and competent in, diverse ICT applications. Of course, any teacher educators continually strive to be responsive to developments and innovations in education within and beyond their discipline.

To understand the strategies of professional development it is important to understand how they are embedded in the broader context of the planning and implementation of ICTs in teacher education.

Teacher educators need to develop competence in the core themes of: pedagogy, collaboration and networking, technical competence, and social issues. This needs to be done within the local and global cultural contexts of: lifelong learning, leadership and vision, and planning and management of change.

For example, a growing number of pre-service teacher education programmes in the USA have employed the ISTE technology standards, and ISTE describes the best of these programmes on the ISTE web site. One such programme was initiated at the University of Texas at Austin, where the teacher educators expert in ICTs have actively planned and promoted the professional development of their colleagues and facilitated the management of change.

The culture is one in which all participants respect the leadership and vision provided by the dean and the college's technology support centre. The current programme evolved from the experiences gained in working with the teacher education faculty. It underscores the importance of learning from the mistakes, as well as the successes, in implementing professional development.

For example, a faculty development workshop was held to teach faculty to use a tool to incorporate web-based elements into their teaching. An initial training session was offered that provided the faculty with an extensive demonstration of the full range of capabilities of the tool. The faculty participants left the two-hour session with cognitive overload and little that they could immediately apply to their courses. Based on this experience, another workshop was designed that focused on a few useful applications that faculty could incorporate into their instruction.

The teacher educators were asked to bring class syllabi and selected course resources to the workshop. The teacher educators learned how to post these materials online in WebCT and set up online class discussions. After the teacher educators had time to see how this worked in practice with their students, a second workshop was provided to help them consider appropriate ways to facilitate collaboration and networking, along with the social issues that might arise in using these methods. These redesigned workshops were highly successful and led to ongoing faculty development.

This effort was successful because this strategy permitted the teacher educators to gain new information about the software within a pedagogical approach that addressed their immediate concerns, and allowed them to pilot the approach and evaluate their efforts. A similar strategy works for other widely used software application tools, such as word processing and desktop publishing.

Professional development for ICTs in teacher education is ongoing, as denoted by the theme of lifelong learning. Successful models for professional development must reflect this dynamic nature by building capacity rather than teaching skills. Reciprocal mentoring is an example of a professional development model that builds capacity within an organization.

In US, Iowa State University has an award-winning programme of teacher education and supports this excellence by providing professional development in ICTs for its teacher educators and the in-service teachers who work with students. Over a decade ago, the course Technology and Teacher Education was established to provide graduate students with an internship experience.

Many of these students become teacher educators who are expert in ICTs. These students mentored teacher educators in ICT skills and, in return, the teacher educators mentored the students in their profession. The graduate students ' advisor, who strategically selected or negotiated the participation of teacher educators, facilitated and planned the interaction.

Over the years, the balance moved from encouragement of reluctant teacher educators to participate, to the strategic choice of participants from a long list of volunteers. Similarly, the context and culture became increasingly akin to a sociable family that supports one another; an organization in which members learn from one another while collaborating and networking. The mentoring course takes place in the fall semester.

Technical competence is purposefully developed slowly, to keep pace with the emerging confidence and autonomy levels of the teacher educator. The graduate students' advisor insists that mentoring graduate students assist the teacher educator to engage with ICTs, rather than allow the teacher educator to delegate the ICT tasks to the student mentor.

ICT applications used in instruction are favoured over those for research, so that the mentoring graduate student can support and experience the development of pedagogic competence. The mentor pairs are expected to engage in many rich conversations as they work together, covering diverse themes and competencies, including social issues with ICTs and discipline specific topics.

Toward the end of the semester, the teacher educators join the mentors ' class for a celebration of their collaborative professional and course development. At this time the teacher educators are exposed to a wide range of ICT applications, cultures, and contexts, and reflect on the four themes and competencies.

A number of states and regions have engaged in a renewal of education. Part of their strategy includes ICTs as a catalyst. However, ICT use is not, in itself, a useful goal. According to a study by the Organization for Economic Co-Operation and Development (OECD) (in preparation), ICTs can be viewed as neutral, i.e., they may support both effective and ineffective education. Effective plans must include strategic objectives and educational vision to inform the use of ICTs for educational renewal.

Leadership and vision are an even more important theme at this transformative level of ICT use in teacher education. Below is an eclectic mix of illustrations to inform professional development planning at the regional and national levels. The framework is used to analyze the mix of themes and competencies that may be developed by particular strategies at the regional, national and international level.

Project InTent was the first national initiative to integrate ICTs into pre-service teacher education. It took place in England between 1989 and 1992, following increasing pressure to prepare teachers before they started practising in schools. The national association of ICT teacher educators published a survey that identified the lack of resources and support for their work.

This first national programme to integrate ICTs into pre-service teacher education requested proposals. Five different types of institutions in England were selected to represent the different types of teacher education organizations. Periodic visits to each organization by the coordinator provided her opportunities to act both as a leader and a mentor for all ICT teacher educators.

An inclusive learning community developed that supported the adoption of a participative action research approach by all project participants and other stakeholders.The project established and published a special journal series called 'Developing information technology in teacher education.' In this way, the project adopted a collaborative networking approach to organizational development to integrate ICTs into teacher education, and the five institutions reinforced each other's commitment to serve the pedagogic needs of all their colleagues, regardless of discipline or approach to content.

There was never any doubt of the aim: colleagues modelling excellent practice with ICTs as they taught methods and content-specific topics. The consortium worked through technical and social issues while integrating ICTs into courses for pre-service teachers, and they supported action research analysis of their own and their colleagues ' professional development while planning and managing change.

One particularly innovative approach to support transfer into school-based practice was to bring an elementary class into the primary base at one of the universities. This practice teaching was intensively supported with lectures, equipment, software, and technical support.

All the teacher educators and support staff received ICT professional development to facilitate a rich environment of good educational practice. Students were able to practice teaching in pairs with a group of four children. This strategy may be particularly appropriate at early stages of ICT adoption in a region where there are few resources and little ICT practice in local schools.

In US, the new government requirement for ICTs in pre-service teacher education provided ample justification for change and an argument for expanding resources in teacher education. The national project leader contributed to institutional development through her research of organizational change, informed by structured interviews of strategically important people. This gathering of evidence was both action and research, because the act of interviewing prompted these people to reflect on ICTs and their place in their organization.

In 1999, educators and policy-makers in the United States recognized the growing crisis in teacher retention and recruitment. The need to develop capacity for ICTs in teacher education within universities and colleges was informed by several research studies in teacher education, undertaken by leading ICT teacher educators with support of their professional societies. It became clear that the improvement of pre-serv-ice teacher education would be an effective use of resources, particularly at a time when schools were losing a high percentage of teachers within five years.

The resources to initiatives that were already using ICTs in innovative ways to enable them to share their expertise in building capacity across a large geographic area. Some of the catalyst projects developed high-quality resources to support the infusion of ICTs into teacher education, such as multimedia case studies of ICTs in schools and universities, and software to assist reflective practice, many of which can be accessed on the Internet.

In addition, in collaboration with the only international society specializing in ICTs in teacher education, a new online journal was established to promote discussion and development, with autonomy for sections edited by relevant content areas.

In Chile, the national ICT initiative is called Enlaces .In common with all of the cited examples of good practice, the design was informed and led by ICT experts, and in this case, the team came from a leading university centre, the Instituto de Informatica Educativa of the Universidad de La Frontera.

The centre conceived the initiative and has played a central role in the development of the Enlaces programme since 1993. In conjunction with the Ministry of Education, it is responsible for the national coordination of the Enlaces Educational Network. The

Institute also conducts research and development activities to support the use of information and communication technology in the network's schools.

The centre was informed by scholarly research in this area, and at least one of the ICT teacher educators undertook a doctoral degree on this topic with leading experts in the University of London Institute of Education. To inform early stages of development and ongoing evaluation the Enlaces initiative drew on a wide range of international consultants in ICTs in education, as well as this close doctoral level supervision. The majority of ICT teacher educators in Enlaces were drawn from 24 universities, which became known as the Technical Assistance Network.

This network was built upon a strategic alliance between the Ministry of Education and universities across the country. The Technical Assistance Network's mission was to train teachers and provide them with technical and educational support. Six universities, designated as Regional Centres, served as coordinators, managing Enlaces activities and teacher training in a particular geographical area of the country. They also carried out applied research in the field of educational ICTs.

One of the fundamental premises of the Enlaces programme was that merely supplying information technology to schools is not enough to bring about significant changes in the quality of education.

Although ICTs can potentially simplify and enhance the learning process in all subject areas and in some cases act as a catalyst for innovation, additional efforts such as teacher training and support -must be done in order to produce sustainable changes in pedagogical practices and student learning outcomes.

Information and communication technologies are tools to be used by all participants in the educational process: students, teachers, school administrators, parents, and sponsors; thus, great emphasis was placed on teacher training and the development of a technical assistance network.

The notions that learning computer skills is an end in itself and only experts can use ICTs were rejected. The goal is to not only equip schools with computers, but also to connect them with each other and the world through an educational network, thus enabling schools to exchange ideas and experiences regardless of their location. This goal also addresses one of the Chilean Educational Reform's key objectives: increasing equity in educational opportunity for all Chilean students.

No single formula can be applied uniformly to all schools, and the uses to which computers and networks are put will depend upon each school's educational projects, needs, and social, cultural, and geographical environment. These considerations, combined with the enthusiasm and initiative of teachers, administrators and students across the country, have often led to surprising results, with broader and deeper implications than those foreseen by the programme.

Enlaces reached 100% of the secondary schools and 50% of the primary schools by 2000, thus covering 90% of the school population. Within this group, Enlaces created an advanced group of ICT-using teachers in 51 schools from different areas of the country. The schools provided local reference sites to demonstrate ICT practice embedded in the local context and culture.

Enlaces equipped these schools with more computers, technical support, and pedagogical assistance than the regular schools, with the expectation that they would become field-based ICT teacher education sites. As a result, these schools formed the core of the collaborative professional development activities that occurred through the Internet.

Furthermore, external evaluations showed that many of the teachers believed that communications via computers in their classes had improved the quality of the teaching-learning process. Two major challenges revealed by these evaluations are the need to supply schools with more computers and a greater variety of educational software, and the concern among teachers about their heavy unpaid workload. The participating schools gained greater prestige in their communities, which translated into increases in enrolment (increased income via larger subsidies).

School officials also valued the increase in equity that occurred as a result of the project's providing equipment that schools otherwise would not have been able to acquire and the coun-try-wide spread of free access to Internet resources. The project also produced improvements in parents ' perception of their schools' performances, which facilitates the learning and teaching process.

From a more global perspective, the evaluations made by the World Bank and the Agency for International Development praise the Enlaces project as one of the most successful programmes in Chile's efforts at educational reform. An important point in this positive evaluation is that the project has expanded its coverage to the national level without sacrificing quality or equity.

Among the factors in this success, the evaluations mention the programme's focus on teachers, the construction of a social network of educators and pupils facilitated by user-friendly technology and decentralized support, and respect for participating schools ' autonomous decisions in the use of the programme's technologies.

The evaluations also emphasize the high quality of the project's technical and administrative team, which has maintained a balanced mix of a clear vision, flexibility, and creativity in the face of new educational challenges and fast-changing technology.

Intel Corporation has launched an international initiative to provide professional development resources to teacher educators in several countries. The programme is based on the Intel Teach to the Future programme begun January 2000 in the United States. The original programme provided training to in-service teachers on the integration of computer technology into teaching and learning.

University faculty who worked with this in-service programme were so impressed by the quality and depth of the pedagogy and materials that they worked with Intel to develop a version of the programme that can be used at the university level with pre-service teachers.

Since then, the materials and curricula have been adapted to thirteen different languages including Spanish, Portuguese, English (British and US), Chinese, Hindi, Japanese, Korean, Urdu (Pakistan), German, Polish, Hebrew, and Russian. As a result, the programme is currently used in teacher preparation programmes in Argentina, Brazil, Canada, China, Costa Rica, Germany, India, Ireland, Italy, Mexico, Taiwan, United Kingdom, and the United States. There are plans to use Intel Teach to the Future in eleven additional countries within the next two years.

The ultimate goal of the Intel Teach to the Future programme is to engage elementary and secondary students in culturally and pedagogically appropriate learning experiences that are enhanced by using computers. "The core focus of this curriculum is to ensure that technology is used successfully to improve student learning. "Teachers are guided to develop face-to-face, student-centred activities that model effective use of technology for teaching and learning.

The Intel Teach to the Future pre-service curricula are designed so that teacher educators and pre-service teachers can use it in a variety of learning Settings. Materials include paper and digital (CD-ROM) resources as well as Web support. Participants learn to use and integrate all three types of resources in their teaching and learning. Topics covered include:

— Developing and teaching technology-enhanced curricula

— Locating and evaluating web resources

— Copyright and citing of sources

— Designing and creating multimedia presentations, desktop-published products, and web sites

— Designing and creating teacher support materials

— Developing plans for project implementation

— Project development and assessment

For many teachers this involves a shift in approach from lecturer and expert to facilitator and learner. Examples created by participants are included with programme materials to assist other pre-service teachers as they develop their own plans and resources. Participants are encouraged to adapt these examples so that they reflect their knowledge of their own cultures. As local teachers develop new examples, they are added to the resource packet for their specific country. This adds relevance and role modelling, and encourages collaboration among pre-service teachers, their colleagues, and university faculty.

# 5

# Lifelong Learning

The crucial role of teachers in the attainment of Education For All (EFA) was underscored by the World Conference on EFA. In this regard, the training of teachers was identified in subsequent meetings as the most important strategy and the biggest challenge in the global struggle to improve the level and quality of student learning.

As EFA seeks to provide lifelong education for all, so must teachers themselves strive to become lifelong learners. It is assumed that quality teacher training leads to quality education in the classroom. If teachers are provided adequate and effective in-service training, then students have better chances of learning more and performing more efficiently.

This is not to say that continuing teacher education is the sole factor influencing teacher performance and, consequently, student achievement. It is, however, a significant variable in the improvement of teaching practices and learning outcomes.

An increasing concern over the quality of teacher education and its effects on student learning led UNESCO and UNDP, with the support of the education officials of the nine high-population countries (E-9), to embark on an inter-regional study on innovative teacher training.

With the end in view of further improving education in general and teacher education in particular, best examples of in-service teacher training in the nine countries were selected. These examples were documented and analysed in order to bring to the attention of various stakeholders in education some experiences and methodologies that can be replicated and applied on a wider scale.

Each programme is described from an analytical framework based on Stufflebeam's (1971) Context-Input-Process-Product (CIPP) model. Context takes into account the programme rationale (including the conditions that provided the basis for establishing the programme); the environment within which the programme operates; the programme goals, objectives, and underlying philosophy; and relevant government policy statements.

Input describes the human, fiscal, and material resources: the key players and the structural supports; financial resources and budgetary considerations; available facilities, equipment, and instructional materials.

Process documents the what and how of programme implementation: the topics or themes covered; the activities, strategies, modalities, and standard operating procedures; the programme schedule and format. Product presents the results of the teacher training programme: measurable and nonmeasurable, quantitative and qualitative programme outcomes, based on programme objectives; and evidences of internal and external efficiency.

Bangladesh has been intensifying efforts to expand and improve primary education since her independence in 1971. The country is also committed to attaining the goals of the 1990 World Conference on Education for All and of the World Summit on Children. In line with these international imperatives, Bangladesh seeks to meet the basic learning needs of all her people by making primary education universal and accessible to children, youth, and adults.

Under the National Plan of Action for EFA, Bangladesh had set a target of 95% gross enrolment and 70% completion to be achieved by the year 2000. As of 1995, 92% enrolment and 60% completion had been reached. But the numbers do not reflect the equal emphasis given to the quality of education.

In view of the teachers' important influence on this, Bangladesh is trying to induct teachers with better academic qualifications and provide them with intensive training for one year. This initial one-year training, however, is not enough to ensure quality teaching in the primary schools.

The importance of continuous in-service teacher training is, therefore, greatly felt. Out of a wide variety of innovative inservice training programmes that have been used in the country, the "sub-cluster training" programme has proven to be the most effective and suitable for Bangladesh.

Sub-cluster training is a need-based structured training with abundant flexibility. The programme gathers together 15-20 teachers from a sub-cluster (i.e., four to five primary schools located within a two-kilometer distance) for one-day training sessions scheduled every two months.

The training, conducted by the Assistant Thana (Area) Education Officers (ATEOs), is based on leaflets that deal with teaching methods/problems identified by teachers.

The leaflets touch on the development of pedagogical skills and provide information related to regular duties performed by classroom teachers. The place of training is rotated among the schools within the sub-cluster areas. The system keeps the training focused on the actual school environment.

The programme is an improved version of the cluster-based training first introduced in seven districts in 1983 in Bangladesh on an experimental basis. Cluster training, involving teachers from 15-20 primary schools at a time, sought to enhance the teachers' capability and skills and enable them to use the knowledge gained in improving the quality of classroom instruction.

Because of its perceived fruitfulness, the cluster training programme, consisting of recurring half-day structured sessions, was expanded to cover the whole country in 1986, under the Universal Primary Education (UPE) Project. However, an evaluation study on the effectiveness of this approach subsequently led to a decision that the training be conducted at a sub-cluster level instead, due to some problems and limitations of cluster training. Sub-cluster training aims mainly to:

— improve and update teachers' knowledge of techniques appropriate for different teaching-learning situations

— strengthen the teachers' capability to apply the teaching techniques effectively, and in turn raise the achievement status of the children.

Nearly 2,100 Assistant Thana Education Officers (ATEO) who supervise primary schools conduct the sub-cluster training. There are three to four ATEOs in a thana (sub-district). The National Academy for Primary Education (NAPE), provides them training on school management, supervision, and sub-cluster training.

Training modules, popularity known as leaflets, are printed materials on specific problems and issues concerning such topics as classroom teaching, school management, and preparation of low-cost teaching aids. These modules are developed by a Steering Committee headed by the Director General of Primary Education. Thus far, 58 leaflets have been prepared. Other training materials include: chalkboard, push-pin, board, flip-chart, and cards, all provided by UNICEF.

The teachers who attend the sub-cluster training are given only some refreshments during training sessions. The government has recently decided, however, to give TK 800 for expenses incurred in the conduct of the training. A day-long structured training session is organized once every two months. The training activities include:

— a demonstration lesson given by a teacher of the school where the training takes place;

— constructive criticism of the demonstration lesson by all the teachers; training based on the leaflets;

— presentation and discussion of co-curricular activities to be implemented in the participants' schools; and

— an open discussion session with parents and school managing committee members on problems and emerging concerns.

Using participatory methods and a variety of training materials, they try to make the curriculum relevant to child-centred, activity-based teaching-learning situations. Overall responsibility for the operation of these training programmes lies with the Thana Education Officers (TEOs). The sub-cluster system answers the need for institutionalized in-service training for primary school teachers.

Through this programme, a teacher now gets a total of six days of training in a year. The involvement of the school managing committee and local community leaders in the open discussion sessions enables the teachers to solve school problems locally in cooperation with them. The parents' participation, likewise, has led to their taking greater interest in school affairs.

The teachers are now observed to be using teaching aids in the classroom more often than before. Some of the major innovative features of the programme are:

— use of an existing network (from central to cluster level) to facilitate programme implementation and keep training costs low

— use of training modules dealing with teacher-identified topics and problems

— development of co-curricular activities based on local needs and resources

— involvement of parents and School Managing Committee members

— participatory training methods

— variety of training materials

— stress on the use of teaching aids in the demonstration lesson.

Sub-cluster training has become almost an institutionalized system covering all the aspects of teaching (e.g. subjects, pedagogy, management, and social mobilization). For this reason, Bangladesh is giving more importance to it. One post of deputy director and assistant director, with several education officers under the training branch of the Directorate of Primary Education, are assigned to look after the entire affairs of sub-cluster training in the country.

A two-day orientation programme on sub-cluster training has recently been given to all the DPEOs and TEOs so that they can oversee and guide the ATEOs properly in improving the quality of training. Perceiving the role of primary education in achieving sustainable and economic development, Bangladesh hopes, through this in-service training programme, to make teachers more responsive to the real life needs of the learners.

Brazil's practice of innovative in-service teacher training takes place in Ijuí, located in the southernmost state of Rio Grande do Sul. The municipality has about 76,000 inhabitants, 83% of whom live in urban areas. It is an important regional centre with an agriculturally based economy, a GNP of approximately US $440 million and a per capita income of US $5,760.

The Municipal Board of Education and Culture (hereinafter referred to as SMEC or the Board) is responsible for the education of approximately 5,700 students in 14 urban and 23 rural schools. Since 1983,

SMEC has been committed to improving the quality of education. Following the prevailing political ideology at the time, which considered the school as a special locus to promote social change, SMEC invested heavily in in-service teacher development as a means of making this possible.

The Northwestern Regional University of the State of Rio Grande do Sul preserves the tradition of high quality public teaching, with its work rooted in local reality. Its goal is to improve the quality of public education. In-service teacher development in Ijuí is a partnership between the Municipal Board and UNIJUÍ. The former organizes multiple and systematic actions carefully so that all Board teachers can be involved in continuing education.

The latter provides training and support to municipal school teachers, principals, and coordinators. The partnership offers the teachers various training activities (e.g., periodic meetings and consultations), special courses or seminars, as well as opportunities to carry out their role as agents and authors of their practice (e.g., writing backup texts and materials).

The training programme is developed according to a yearly generating theme, divided into two-month subthemes. These are used to integrate the grade activities and link the different subjects. The programme is being implemented in a culture characterized by collective participation among individuals and groups and the strong presence of the Catholic Church.

It tries to address problems such as: the rural children's difficulty in reaching school; the existence of too many small one-teacher schools with multigrade classes; the reduced number of rural schools due to migration and lower birth rates; the increasing suburban population. The programme aims to:

— reduce student drop-out rate;

— ensure that children from rural areas can get to and attend school;

— restore general confidence in the teachers' capacity to offer high quality teaching, so that students will stay longer and be successful at school. SMEC activities are guided by the following premises:

— belief in the teachers' capacity to fashion and develop their school;

— respect for diversity of ideas and social participation of groups;

— belief in the school's competence and

— ability to design its own political-pedagogical project;

— decentralization of pedagogic decisions and actions.

In order to improve and ensure quality, the SMEC has been taking actions directed at:

a) educators' qualification and professional improvement;

b) the Board's political-pedagogic project;

c) redeeming popular culture;

d) strengthening partnerships with other school systems and segments of society;

e) implementing School Councils

f) Teachers' Career Plan and salary increase;

g) election of school principals;

h) budget allocation for education; and

i) appointment of a Municipal Education Council.

Financial resources for the programme are taken from the budget allotted for education. Control of the budget, however, is the responsibility of the financial body of the municipality. Involved in the programme are UNIJUÍ professors and personnel from the SMEC administrative and pedagogic sections. The Board has 481 educators, including 27 principals and vice-principals elected for a two-year term, and 19 school coordinators appointed by the principal, who act as staff developers and teacher trainers.

The training covers content areas and learning theories. It also allows teachers to conceive of more dynamic and creative teaching strategies, based on their interactions with the Board and on their daily school practice. Principals study and discuss pedagogic approaches, participative management, and administrative issues. School coordinators raise questions about the school's role, learning theories, and teachers' pedagogic actions.

The programme follows a "back-and-forth" process, wherein teachers first discuss their practices, questions, and needs among themselves, then with SMEC and UNIJUÍ consultants, and back again with their peers. This process enables the teachers to design their grade curriculum experimentally, set up goals, define basic concepts, and implement theory-based projects.

All programmes are evaluated every year. The ensuing results allow for adjustments in the following year's programme. Format Schools organize their activities around the teacher development courses, as these are part of their weekly working hours. These schedules allow different groups to hold weekly, bimonthly, or monthly meetings at the Board offices or at the school itself, according to the needs of the teachers, principals, and school coordinators.

The programme has succeeded in redeeming the teachers' credibility through their authorship of various educational materials. It has also resulted in school-community integration, citizen formation, and increased self-esteem of rural workers. Teacher assistance has become part of the routine of the school, the Board, UNIJUÍ, and the town's life.

University teachers are now more aware of the needs of the municipal schools. Records show that the 1994 dropout rate was down to 3% (from 8% in 1987). Retention rate was still significant, at 16%, although down from the 1987 record of almost 20%. The novel features of the programme include:

— the SMEC-UNIJUÍ partnership

— the goal not only of teaching the regular subjects of the first grades, but also of creating and developing citizenship practices among students.

— municipal schools becoming objects of research

— teacher training as a living example of the political will of two institutions committed to being of service to their community

— horizontal and reciprocal relationships, enhancing confidence, respect, tolerance and

— self-esteem, and innovative pedagogic ideas

— autonomy for pedagogic decisions

The success of Ijuí's in-service teacher development stems largely from the consensus of the teachers, SMEC, and UNIJUÍ about the importance of continuing education. Through training, the teachers have acquired more thorough and extensive knowledge, enabling them to enrich and reformulate their practice to make their classes more meaningful. Teaching is thus focused on local needs, helping people develop roots and enhancing development.

Teacher training schools in China, strengthened and rebuilt in the early 1980s, have been a major base for the in-service training of primary school teachers. There are at present 2,153 such institutions, with almost one for each county and city district. From 1980 to 1995, more than two million teachers were trained in these schools. In the first four years, training focused on enabling teachers to master subject matter and develop basic teaching competence.

From 1984 to 1990, the training objective was to help unqualified teachers obtain a diploma of secondary normal education. As a result of the 15-year endeavour, the percentage of unqualified primary school teachers decreased from 53% to 12% of the 5.664 million teaching force in 1995. Given this condition, the training priority for most parts of China has changed from training for qualification (diploma of secondary normal education) to continuing education.

Continuing education is offered through various programmes to serve the professional needs of all qualified teachers. The programmes include training for the following: new teachers, key teachers, teachers in new teaching posts, and potential key teachers, with emphasis on the first two.

Continuing education of primary school teachers in teacher training institutions is guided by the following documents issued by the State Education Committee (SEDC): "Suggestions on Conducting Continuing Education for Primary School Teachers" (1991), "Suggestions on Strengthening the Training for Key Teachers of Primary Schools" (1993), and "Suggestions on Conducting the Training for New Primary School Teachers on Probation" (1994). Based on these national policies, many provinces and cities have formulated their own policies and regulations to suit regional situations.

Both urban and rural models of successful training programs have been developed. The shift in training emphasis to continuing education for primary school teachers was based on the following factors:

— the poor professional performance of teachers who are qualified only in terms of their diplomas

— major changes in basic education in China (e.g.; from examination-oriented to quality-oriented education;

— from educating the gifted to educating all children; from purely intellectual education to holistic development;

— from subject-centred to child-centred teaching;

— from unified standard requirements to differential aptitude treatment)

— educational reforms and curriculum innovations requiring updated teaching competence.

The underlying philosophy of in-service teacher training is the idea of lifelong education. Its purposes are:

a) to increase the teachers' professional morality and teaching capacity;

b) to enable all teachers to develop professional qualities based on their own current levels; and

c) to foster key teachers and specialists in primary education.

The legal basis of the SEDC policies is the "Teachers' Law of People's Republic of China." This law stipulates that participating in further learning and training is a teacher's right and duty. It also states that educational bureaus at all levels of the Chinese government are responsible for laying out long-term training plans. It designates teacher training schools as the implementing institutions for the task of teacher training.

The leaders of the teacher training schools have overall responsibility for the training process: training design, activity planning, curriculum development, teaching, and evaluation. Trainers are both from within and outside the training institutions. Full-time trainers are teachers from the teacher training schools.

Part-time trainers, who constitute the larger bulk of trainers, are usually taken from the staff of the teaching-research section of county education bureaus, outstanding primary school teachers, specialists from educational technology centres and educational research institutes, and university professors in primary education.

In-service teacher training is regarded as a local education undertaking. Expenses for continuing education are therefore taken from local education funds. In addition, a certain percentage of extra funds for teacher education allocated by the central government may be used for continuing education. The financial situation differs, however, from place to place.

As a major base of in-service training for primary school teachers, teacher training schools are equipped with: a teaching building, library, laboratory, teaching equipment, dormitories, and dining rooms. Where physical and financial resources are inadequate, some provinces resort to integrating and sharing available resources from several units (e.g., teaching-research section, educational technology centre, teacher training school).

The training materials developed by experts or full-time teachers reveal regional diversity and creative innovations. The content prescribed by the SEDC covers the following general aspects: professional ethics and political education; educational theories, curriculum and pedagogy, educational practice and basic teaching skills; new knowledge and technology; vocational knowledge and skills useful for community development and indigenous education.

In practice, the content is very flexible and varies for the different types of trainees (i.e., new teachers, key teachers or potential teachers). Training activities take place both within and outside of teacher training schools.

Various methods emphasize the combination of theory with practice, and learning by doing. In school-based training, key teachers and senior staff of primary schools act as peer coaches and tutors. Trainers from teacher training school supervise all primary school activities.

Different formats are adopted for the learning activities: class teaching in teacher training schools, large group instruction in the town school classroom, small group study within the village school, self-study, and correspondence learning. Some provinces have introduced indigenous practices such as organizing teaching demonstration teams composed of trainees who excel during training and providing advanced follow-up training for young, outstanding, potential trainers.

The duration of the training programmes varies, from half a day to three months. Credit system is used for the accumulation of training hours and completion of learning content. Assessment of trainees' performance emphasizes the theory-practice combination. Pilot programmes in many training schools in China have shown successful results, as reported in national journals and meetings. Results include demonstration of effective teaching skills and increased professional awareness and capacity.

Primary school principals have expressed satisfaction with their teachers' progress and achievements in teaching after the training.

Moreover, the training process itself has also contributed to school quality improvement and teaching reforms. There is likewise a lower teacher turnover rate. Through continuing education, "local born and local grow up" teachers are able to become "permanent" teachers and key teachers, serving as a major force to improve basic education in rural and mountain areas.

Continuing education in teacher training schools in China has six innovative features: (a) a training-for- all-teachers orientation; (b) the use of part- time trainers from local communities; c) short-term and part-time training programmes; (d) adaptation to local conditions to meet the variety of training needs (e) integration of training, teaching research and educational reforms into one process; and (f) delivery of training down to township schools in rural areas.

Teacher training schools have paid much attention to rural areas, where most primary school teachers are working. By reaching out to the grassroots units, the teacher training schools have therefore provided training where it is most needed and where the resources are most inadequate.

Two major forces account for the success of the continuing education programmes offered by teacher training schools: the importance attached by the educational authorities at each level in China to this mission of teacher training schools; the validity of the training content and flexibility of training arrangements.

In Egypt, as in any other country, individuals are seen as the most important resources for achieving higher rates of social and economic development. With the emergence of the Egyptian constructive revolution in 1952, the government regarded education as the foundation for rapid economic growth and social change.

It also looked at education as a major objective of the creation of an enlightened and democratic society. Consistent with these outlooks, the government adopted a national policy of free education at all educational levels and equal educational opportunity for everyone in society.

In order to realize these theoretical ideas, the Egyptian government reorganized the public educational system, classifying it into eight years of compulsory basic education (five-year elementary stage and three-year preparatory stage) and three years of secondary stage. It also increased state expenditure on education and increased the number of schools and students in the different educational stages.

As a result of the rapid increase in the number of schools and students at the pre-university level, there has been a persistent need for a large number of academically and professionally qualified teachers. Because of an insufficient supply of such teachers, however, the Ministry of Education has been forced to hire a large number of unqualified teachers to cater to the needs of all educational stages.

In spite of their importance as the cornerstone of the educational process, elementary stage teachers have long been neglected in terms of their professional, academic and socio-economic status. The Egyptian government has therefore developed educational policies during the last three decades in order to overcome their problems.

One solution has been the organization of in-service training programmes in order to improve the teachers' academic and professional level. This programme was developed in 1983-84 by the Ministry of Education, in coordination with the Faculty of Education of Ain Shams University and the National Center of Educational Research and Development. Since then, other faculties of education have participated in it.

Up to 1983, the majority of the Egyptian elementary school teachers (numbering about 15,000) were not university graduates. In response to educational reform strategies and the need to help elementary school teachers who only had diplomas in elementary stage training, the Ministry of Education decided to upgrade their professional and academic status.

In order to legitimize this programme, the Supreme Council of Universities issued two decrees in 1983: one granting approval to the programme, the other awarding a bachelor's degree in education to its graduates.

The programme takes the form of in-service training in order to solve many problems such as the shortage of elementary school teachers, transportation, and overcrowding in the faculties of education. It was envisioned that all elementary school teachers throughout the country would have received their degrees within ten years from the programme's inception. The in-service training programme aims to:

— improve teachers' abilities and skills in teaching,

— managing, and participating effectively in

— classroom and school activities;

— develop teachers' academic and professional competencies; and

— promote teachers' capacities to be more active participants in the development of their society, the environment, the educational system, and the teaching profession.

The Ministry of Education is fully responsible for the financial support of organization and supervision of the programm. In addition, applicants have to pay tuition fees ranging from EL 50 to 70 per academic year. The programme falls into four levels that correspond to four academic years. Each level consists of three semesters; winter, spring and summer, with the latter spent for practical studies. The study plan contains two sets of courses. The first set is professional, which includes courses in education, psychology, and teaching methods. These courses are obligatory for all teacher trainees and aim at improving their professional knowledge and practice. The second set of courses is related to academic knowledge. It is composed of two academic specializations: (a) Arabic language, religious education, and social studies or (b) mathematics and science. Applicants select their academic specialization at the beginning of the second level.

Most of these are required, and some are elective. The total number of contact hours needed for graduation is about 200. Although this programme depends primarily on self-learning and distance education, instruction and consultation through radio and TV are also available. In addition, there are weekly discussion meetings with faculty staff members at the centres near their workplace. These meetings take place the evening as well as during the weekends.

Since 1994, however, some changes have been instituted in the programme. The TV and radio programmes of instruction were discontinued for technical reasons. Meetings were transferred from the centres, to the faculties of education, to cut down costs and keep participants in touch with the faculty.

In the current decentralized scheme, each Faculty of Education is responsible for the examination of its participants at the end of each semester. The programme has resulted in the upgrading of the professional level of participants through their attainment of a university degree. Teachers are observed to have become more active in the profession, and to have benefited from their exposure to new trends.

The major innovation of this programme is the linkage between the Ministry of Education and faculties of education for the in-service training of teachers. Other features introduced in the early stages of implementation of the programme were the self-learning and distance education mode, supplemented by weekly discussion meetings with faculty staff members at centres close to the participants' workplace and residence.

The programme of upgrading the elementary school teachers to university level has shown success in certain aspects of the educational process. There is a need, however, to review some of its components in order to find solutions to problems raised by its participants with respect to regulations, curricula, textbooks, and the assessment system.

P rimary education in India has come of age. Massive and commendable efforts made by the central and state governments have resulted in tremendous gains in enrolment of primary school students. The enrolment at the primary level, which was only 19.2 million in 1950-51, went up to 109 million in 1995. During the same period, the enrolment at the upper primary level went up from 3.1 million to 40.2 million.

These encouraging enrolment figures pale in comparison to the dropout rate. Nearly 40% of students get pushed out of the educational system by the time they reach Class VI. This mixed picture forces a rethinking about what ails elementary education. One possible reason for the non-attainment of universal elementary education lies in the parents' and teachers' failure to understand the needs and interests of the primary school child.

Without basic knowledge about child development, parents and teachers may inadvertently be creating inhibitive and restrictive environments that smother the child's growth. As a consequence of this, children develop negative attitudes toward schooling and eventually drop out. It is here where the role of guidance comes in.

In this regard, the National Council of Educational Research and Training (NCERT) has been offering an Advanced Diploma Course in guidance and counselling at the postgraduate level. The programme, which has been going on for about two decades, has so far touched only the tip of the problem. Guidance in primary schools still remains largely unattended.

The Certificate in Guidance is an attempt to orient teachers and parents in matters relating to child guidance, with the end in view of bringing about the child's comprehensive and holistic development. The programme focuses on the identification of needs and problems related to physical, social, and emotional issues of the children.

The CIG is based on the philosophy of institutional collaboration. It synergizes the strengths of two institutions: the NCERT, which develops curriculum frameworks for all levels of school education, and the Indira Gandhi Open University (IGNOU), which is dedicated to open distance education.

The programme was conceived in the context of the 1990 Jomtien conference emphasis on the importance of primary education and children's basic learning needs. It was hoped that if teachers and parents properly understood the primary school child, they would undertake actions to promote the children's retention in schools and facilitate their academic achievement. This resulted into a collaborative project between NCERT and IGNOU, with NCERT designing the curriculum and IGNOU offering the course through its Regional and Study Centres.

The course is directed toward helping parents and teachers:

1. understand the elementary school child
2. identify and understand problems relating to learning and the socio-emotional development of elementary school children
3. understand concepts and processes related to guiding school children at the elementary level, and
4. take preventive measures to overcome learning and socio-emotional problems of elementary school children.

The CIG course is open to: regular teachers, individuals who have passed the senior secondary course or matriculation examination, parents, and persons from non-government organizations. Candidates must be at least 21 years old. Priority is given to primary and elementary school teachers.

The 1994 statistics show that nearly 60% of the 801 participants were in the age range of 21-35 years. Females constituted 68%; the employed students were 51.7%; and 74% came from urban areas. The programme is covered by a Memorandum of Understanding between NCERT and IGNOU, and is therefore assured of financial support from these institutions, both fully financed by the Central Government. Students pay a fee of Rs. 300/-, which is valid up to two years from the date of admission. The study and support materials, jointly developed by NCERT and IGNOU, include audio-video programmes and self-instructional printed modules.

Information about the programme, in Hindi and English, is advertised in newspapers and on radio and television. It is likewise available in the IGNOU Head Office (New Delhi) as well as in Regional Centres, each of which has Study Centres under it. The programme offers four courses: Understanding the Elementary School Child, Facilitating Growth and Development, Guiding Children's Learning, and Guiding the Socio-emotional Development of Children. The instruction design uses a multimedia approach to teaching, with the following components:

a) self-learning materials,

b) face-to-face contact sessions,

c) academic counselling in regional centres,

d) audio-video programmes, and

e) inbuilt exercise and assignments.

Soon after enrolment, the candidate receives instructional materials and a time schedule for counselling sessions. Academic counselling is provided on Saturdays and Sundays in the Study Centres. Counsellors, who are child guidance experts, try to answer students' queries and tackle their problems and difficulties.

When the learning materials are given to students, they are advised to read learning materials very closely and critically. They are also told to do all assignments (two per course) given in the printed booklets. Successful completion of all the eight assignments within the stipulated time is required of students who sit for final examination for all the four courses at one time.

Although the course is designed for six months, students have the option to stagger it over two years. They are also at liberty to appear in all the examinations conducted by the University during the year, provided they have met the minimum time prescribed.

The students are regularly evaluated through exercises within each unit, periodic assignment, and term-end examination. Because of the flexibility in the CIG evaluation system, where students have four chances to appear for examinations over a period of two years, it becomes difficult to calculate pass percentage.

The records show, however, that 1,081 students have completed the course. The programme has succeeded in making parents and teachers aware of the need to accept children as they are. It has gradually and subtly made the point that holistic growth is more important than mere cognitive growth.

The CIG has likewise tacitly given an important message: that at the primary level, the development of the child's cognitive, affective, and psycho-motor domains is a joint responsibility of parents and teachers.

The strengths and resources of NCERT and IGNOU are brought together to provide the needed facilities, student support services, and management system. Its focus on holistic child development and on the partnership of parents and teachers in this task are also welcome innovations.

The task of teacher upgrading and in-service training in Indonesia is a formidable one. There are altogether 1.770 million school teachers, 1.2 million of whom are teaching in the primary schools. Approximately one million of these primary school teachers have to be upgraded, in view of a government policy, issued in 1989, which requires teachers at this level to possess at least a Diploma II degree.

The new curriculum of 1994 further demands retraining and/or refresher courses of qualified teachers, to orient them to the new approach and structure as well as to the new textbooks and teaching materials.

There are three basic types of in-service teacher training offered by the Directorate General for Primary and Secondary Education: refresher, upgrading, and career training. These programmes are implemented using various mechanisms. No single in-service training modality, however, can claim to have solved all of the teachers' lack of qualification and professionalism.

Nevertheless, considering the massive teacher training requirements, it appears that the face-to-face conventional approach alone is not enough to fill the need. On the other hand, distance education, using printed learning materials or modules, has reached less than 200,000 teachers within six years of its initiation.

With these two training modalities, it will take 25 years to complete the upgrading programme. Using radio broadcasting for teachers' in-service training seems to show brighter prospects.

The Radio In-service Training (Diklat SRP) is an outgrowth of a pilot project, initiated in 1976, on the use of radio broadcasting for teachers' upgrading. It is a programme for underqualified primary school teachers that will enable them to collect in three years a total of 80 credit points required for teaching at the primary level.

The programme is managed by the Centre of Communication Technology for Education and Culture (Pustekkom), under the Ministry of Education and Culture. Pustekkom being a non-degree granting institution, it collaborates with the Indonesian Open Learning University (Universitas Terbuka; UT).

The broadcast curriculum is therefore currently based on UT's DII Equivalence Programme by Distance Learning. Diklat SRP addresses the need to improve the primary school teachers' professional competence in both teaching method and content. It is meant particularly for those residing in rural and remote places.

The basic programme philosophy is that any improvement of the quality of education should begin with the most critical point, the teachers. It is also assumed that mobilizing available resources can eliminate disparity in educational quality caused by socio-economic and geographical conditions. The main objectives of Diklat SRP are:

(a) improving the teachers' professional competence in both teaching methodology and subject mastery, and

(b) providing the disadvantaged teachers with learning opportunities to help them attain the teaching standard qualification.

Diklat SRP is managed jointly at the central and provincial levels by teams consisting of designated staff from relevant units of the Pustekkom, the Directorate of Primary Education, and the Directorate of Teacher Education. In addition, linkages are established at the provincial level with the national radio networks and the local constituent body of the Ministry of Home Affairs under the provincial Governor.

The instructional team that develops the broadcast programmes consists of curriculum or subject specialists, media specialists, evaluation experts, experienced teachers, scriptwriters, studio teachers or cast, radio producers, and liaison officers.

The programme is financed mainly by the central government, through routine and development budgets. The routine fund is for staff salary, maintenance of building and equipment, and daily operations. The development budget is for the design and production of print and non-print instructional materials or programmes, as well as for supervision and evaluation. The local governments contribute by providing wireless sets to the learning groups.

Teachers participating in the Diklat SRP are required to be active teachers and civil servants (or prospective ones). They should not have been registered as students of the regular, face-to-face DII programme. Instructional materials available for the teachers are mainly in the form of the broadcast lessons and the printed corollary learning materials.

Additional visual materials (e.g., video recordings and sound-slides) are also provided at the local implementation units. In order to invite teachers to participate in the programme, Pustekkom produces and disseminates promotional materials in printed form and radio spots.

Teachers willing to participate in the programme have to form learning groups, one in each school. Group learning activities include listening to the radio programmes (aired 20 minutes twice a day), reading the supplementary printed materials, and discussing the relevant topics. Reports on these activities are sent once a month to the local implementing unit.

Radio scripts and their printed supplementary materials are based on a predetermined Basic Pattern of Teaching and Learning. The supplementary materials contain the lesson's abstract and activity guidelines, including the broadcast timetable. These materials are sent to the learning groups prior to the broadcast of the lessons.

The broadcast lessons are organized into six packages, each one offered for a semester. All problems encountered during individual and group learning are dealt with by visiting supervisors and/or the local implementing unit of Pustekkom in the provinces. Radio feedback in response to these problems is prepared for subsequent local broadcast.

Teachers who are active members of a learning group may participate in the examinations upon the recommendation of their school principal. Performance assessment is prepared by content specialists, with the assistance of test construction experts and technical staff. The actual evaluation is done by and under the supervision of the respective school principals.

The number of teachers participating in the project fluctuates from year to year. Since its initiation in 1992, however, the project has awarded certificates of completion to 345,917 out of a total of 489,572 teachers. This reflects a success rate of approximately 70%.

A short survey indicates, however, that teachers are feeling good about the availability of the programme, because it serves as a morale booster. Based on simple quantitative measures (e.g., the number of lessons produced and broadcast, the number of corollary learning materials prepared and distributed, and the frequency of learning assessment), the programme implementors claim the cost effectiveness of Diklat SRP.

External efficiency is determined comparatively. The programme's operational budget for 1996-97 was roughly $350,000 for 117,432 active learners amounting to less than $3 per teacher. This figure is much lower than the budgets allocated for two other programmes with more or less the same objectives.

The most significant innovative feature of this programme is its use of radio broadcasting as an instructional medium. The process of innovation includes the management of activities, personnel, resources, and learning.

Another novel characteristic of the programme is its philosophical strategy of mobilization of resources. Cooperation of related agencies is solicited, enhanced, and enforced; systematic problem-solving method is applied; and related factors such as finances, time, and personnel are considered.

The success of this in-service training programme can be attributed to the strong political will of the Indonesian government to improve the quality of teachers, the leadership within and outside the programme, and the teachers' acceptance of and confidence in the program.

Broadcasting and telecommunications technology show tremendous potential for educational application. The prospect of applying this programme on a wider scale for teacher upgrading is therefore very bright.

T he problems of education in Mexico have led to several reforms and constant moves to update and modernize teaching methods. The adoption of innovations in education has not been very successful, however.

One basic reason for this is the inadequacy of the methods and contents adopted. The other is the lack of professors who are proficient in the new methods. In Mexico, this is an important factor to consider, given the natural tendency to adopt new methods with few supporting tools. It has been observed, in fact, that several teachers who think they are following a new method are in reality constrained by their own training, traditions, social customs, and ideologies that are resistant to change.

Frequently, the efforts to improve the quality of education focus on certificate courses for teachers. Some research results show, however, that the most important factors that affect improvement are attitude, work, and concrete methodologies applied in the classroom. These are factors not linked with the teachers' academic qualifications.

For these reasons, the education authorities of the state of Veracruz decided to develop the programme "Action Research on Concept and Attitude Formation in Preschool and Primary Education" (IACAE). IACAE is offered to preschool and primary education teachers.

The programme, introduced in 1987, is so organized as to elicit the participation and support of the community in a given zone: professors, supervisors, teachers, children, and parents. Attitude change is achieved through the teachers' involvement in action-research, and their exposure to participatory teaching techniques. The project arose as a response to the following needs:

— restoring the teachers' esteem for their own profession;

— improving the quality of education;

— decreasing the school dropout rates in the state of Veracruz;

— linking the school to the community;

— training teachers as researchers; and improving the terminal efficiency of the primary school students.

Through this programme, the teachers can regain their importance in the community as a major part in the cultural, political, and social life of their students. IACAE aims primarily to develop the teachers' competencies in

(a) promoting a change of attitude in the different instances in the teaching-learning process;

(b) maximizing the use of theory-based pedagogic and dialectical tools in primary and preschool education; and

c) linking the school with the community and with the different participating actors in education.

The end goals are to reduce the school dropout rate, increase the terminal efficiency and quality of education, and foster a better appreciation for the teaching practice by the teachers themselves. In support of the programme, the government has issued policies to establish teacher training and updating courses as well as parents' schools in pilot zones located in urban, suburban, indigenous, and rural areas. Due respect is given to the customs, traditions, and popular culture of the assisted population.

Strategic planning for the institutional setup involves the General Director of Popular Education, a project coordinator, a project technical and implementing team, and assistants. In planning for project development and implementation, this group is joined by the zone colleges, in cooperation with supervisors, teachers, parents, and children. Teachers' participation in the programme is on a voluntary basis.

Financial resources come from state funds for primary education. The budget is based on the Annual Operations Programme that determines the coverage, goals, strategies, and schedule of activities, as well as personnel, physical, and other requirements. Instructional materials include: teaching activities support guide, schoolwork guide, audiovisual aids, organization manual, and self-instructional texts for teachers.

School zones are selected for the project on the basis of indicators such as dropouts, absenteeism, and terminal efficiency, taken in the context of geographic, socio-economic, and cultural factors. The programme content covers, among others: action research methodology; teaching methodology for different subjects; participatory teaching techniques; designing and producing low-cost didactic material; popular education; school-community linking strategies. The five-step process involves:

(a) contracts with community authorities,

(b) participatory diagnosis with the community,

(c) planning of activities,

(d) implementation, and

(e) evaluation.

As a result of the programme, the value of the teaching practice has been reaffirmed. The teachers, trained to be action researchers, are now committed to be change agents. There is also a greater sensitivity to the link between the preschool and primary levels. Attitude change is seen concerning the teaching-learning process and the school-community relationship.

The students' participation as active elements in the teaching-learning process has developed their creativity and critical thinking skills, resulting in improved school work. Extra-classroom friendships have been formed. What is most visible is the programme impact on the community. It has strengthened the school-community linkage and effected adult literacy.

The model offers several innovations in in-service teacher training: the use of action research methods in the formal educational system; the involvement of school authorities, parents, teachers, and children; the stress on attitude as a change agent; and the establishment of a Parents' School and a Professors' College.

This unique approach to teacher formation is valued by the teachers, parents, children, and the community because it allows them to be actors and authors of their own development. It enhances school-community linkages and promotes significant learning built on concepts derived from daily life experiences. The coordination of the educational experiences of preschool and primary students facilitates the children's progress to the next level. Its replicability lies in its adaptability to the local context.

T he declaration of Universal Primary Education in 1976 led to a phenomenal increase in the school population, especially at the primary level, in Nigeria. As of 1993, there were 13.7 million primary school students and about 400,000 teachers.

In spite of government efforts, however, there remains an acute shortage of qualified teachers. If Nigeria is to tackle squarely the problems of education at all levels, then the issue of teachers must be addressed. The solution should be found in providing adequate training and retraining for teachers as long as they are in the education industry.

Such in-service training programmes should take cognizance of the serious economic difficulties that

Nigeria is currently going through, and must be cost-effective. Most in-service teacher training programmes utilize experts from higher (tertiary) institutions or from the Ministry of Education, who normally deliver lectures and teach skills. It must be recognized, however, that in an educational environment, such as a local government area, there are very good teachers in some of the schools.

And yet, not too far from a school with a crop of good teachers are clusters of other schools with teachers who need to improve their teaching skills. An arrangement that could pool these resources together holds promise not only as an economical but also as an innovative and effective scheme.

The Peer In-Service Approach (PISA) is a "self-help" in-service approach that drastically reduces the cost of financing training programmes for teachers within local government areas. It recognizes the skills of good teachers in any locality with a cluster of schools. The expertise of these good teachers is utilized to update other teachers in neighbouring schools in the same area. The good teachers are therefore regarded as "itinerant in-service teachers."

Programmes are arranged as the need arises. The Peer In-Service Approach is based on the belief that primary education is the basis of the formal and non-formal systems. Hence there is a need to lay a solid foundation in such a way that all the children would be taught the basic skills of reading and numeracy. PISA also takes into consideration the declared intentions of government in its National Policy on Education.

Thus, the stakeholders in PISA are: relevant arms of government, classroom teachers at the primary education level, and primary school pupils. As is always in any educational reform, the beneficiaries are the society at large and learners attaining high learning achievement.

In considering in-service teacher training at the primary education level, there is a need for the "expert" to be an "insider" rather than an "outsider." The expert must not only know about the educational environment; there must be evidence of actually experiencing the kind of education being offered at the primary level. PISA experts, because of their familiarity with the local cultural and socio-economic dimensions, can more easily "sell" the training programme to their peers and thus make it more acceptable.

Teachers who attend PISA would be in possession of in-service training materials relevant to the individual needs. There would be a significant reduction in the budget aspects dealing with in-service training of teachers. Pupils' learning achievement will significantly improve.

In-service exposure will provide additional qualification to upgrade the teachers' level. Programme participants consist of teachers from the schools within a vicinity. "Good" schools are selected on the basis of: ownership (private or Federal or special state science schools); quality/quantity of teachers; quality of learning environment.

"Experts" chosen from these schools and who constitute the in-service tutors meet the following criteria: academic qualification; professional qualification; teaching experience (not less than five years); familiarity with local government area (stay in LGA not less than three years); administrative experience (position not less than senior teacher); rating from school principal (high).

They are possible role models for the other teachers. Funding requirements are minimal.

On the basis of needs assessment and situational analyses, "good" schools in a given Local Government Education Authority (LGEA) are identified. From these schools, "experts" in some subject areas are selected. Sensitization/awareness training in the good schools are then conducted. With training materials produced from workshops, the PISA expert teachers first provide in-service training to the teachers in their respective schools and then extend that service to identified schools in the vicinity. These take the form of short-term or long-term focused training, which are non-residential.

Formative and summative evaluation activities are carried out, including assessment of pupils and the educational system. PISA has been adopted in a science programme across Nigeria. Science and technology being considered crucial in the march towards national development, it was decided that children should be introduced to these disciplines in an exciting way.

Project ELSSA [Early Learning Science Series for Africa] was therefore used as the vehicle to propagate PISA. ELSSA as a national project has been introduced through sensitization workshops for teachers in three regions of the country. The effectiveness of PISA is seen in the general improvement of the teachers' educational level and in the achievement of learners who interact with PISA-trained teachers. The latter is measured through the pupils' performance in the ongoing national Monitoring of Learning Achievement (MLA).

It is clear that the most novel feature of PISA is its utilization of the expertise of good teachers for the in-service training of other teachers in nearby schools. This approach gives recognition to the good teachers and thus, in a significant way, raises their self-esteem.

As peers to the other teachers, the good teachers are easily accepted. PISA, as an in-service strategy, has three advantages:

— Firstly, it is a kind of "self-help" project where teachers help other teachers.

— Secondly, it develops high self-esteem in the teachers who act as role models.

— Thirdly, it is proving to be a low-cost approach.

PISA has all the potentials of replicability in all the states of the Federation of Nigeria. And of particular interest is the fact that it can be replicated in other countries within the E-9 Initiative.

It has been established that no teacher, once trained, can be considered fully competent throughout his or her career without taking periodic refresher courses. The Commission on National Education of Pakistan reinforced this idea in 1959 by proposing a mechanism for teachers to have in-service training, at least once every five years.

Two types of institutions, formal and non-formal, have been established to cope with the demand for in-service teacher training. Belonging to the formal type are provincially administered in-service teacher training institutions under the titles of (a) In-service Teacher Training Centres, (b) Education Extension Centres, and (c) Directorate of Staff Development.

Other provincially administered formal institutions are: government colleges of elementary education, which take on in-service teacher training during the vacation period; and the Primary Teachers Alternate Course of Baluchistan, which provides a three-month summer training programme to untrained teachers who have had 10 years of schooling.

Formal training is likewise given through the federally administered and Asian Development Bank-sponsored teacher training project (1993-98), whose targets are the recently appointed teachers of the newly established schools during the project period.

Non-government organizations have also been conducting formal in-service training, through the Teachers Resource Centre in Karachi, and the Project for Rural Primary Teachers of the Ali Institute of Education in Lahore.

Allama Iqbal Open University (AIOU), Islamabad is and has been the only institute providing non-formal in-service teacher training to primary school teachers. The New Primary Teachers Orientation Course (PTOC) is an intensive in-service teacher training programme of 18 weeks that is provided by AIOU using a distance education mode.

It focuses on improving the teachers' practical skills through the adoption of innovative teaching methods. It is given to trained primary school teachers in the service who have had no previous exposure to the new teaching methodology. It is designed to make up for deficiencies in their preparation. AIOU started the old PTOC programme in 1976 upon the request of provincial departments of education. From this time until 1988, it provided an 18-week training programme to about 83,000 untrained primary school teachers through its distance education system.

Like other pre-service and in-service teacher training courses in the country, however, the old PTOC was characterized by a heavy theory-oriented curriculum and an academic bias in the training. It was with this historical background that the new PTOC programme was established with the sponsorship of NORAD for the period of 1992 to 1998.

The programme aims to provide skills-oriented re-training to working primary school teachers-females and males, junior and senior, from rural and urban areas in all the four provinces of Pakistan. The programme is adequately equipped with human, material, and physical resources.

Material resources come in the form of print and non-print media. Printed study materials consist of 18 study units, arranged into six blocks: Expository; Pedagogy; Teaching of Science; Teaching of Mathematics; Language/Humanities; Teaching of Physical Education and Arts and Crafts. The materials are written in the style of self-study distance education, with input from different scholars and primary education experts inside and outside the University.

Electronic media consist of five radio programmes of 15 minutes each, two TV programmes of 30 minutes each, and one 60-minute audio-cassette programme. These are interlinked with the print media according to the basic requirements of the open learning system.

Incentives are given to the trainees in the form of transportation allowance for attendance in the tutorials, workshops, and final examination. Medals, certificates, and scholarships are also awarded to those who complete the programme with distinction. PTOC graduates likewise get preferential admission to AIOU's CT and BEd level teacher training programmes.

The following eight teaching competencies are stressed in the programme: introduction of the lesson, presentation, effective questioning, listening, participation, recapitulation, teacher liveliness, and closure. These are developed through the microteaching approach with the use of a video camera. The trainees are required to attend two workshops, for a total of nine full days, for practical demonstrations, planning and presentation of lessons. Aside from these, nine fortnightly tutorials of one hour each are provided for face-to-face contacts between the trainees and the tutors.

Activities in these tutorials are all student-centred. The trainees are given opportunities for video recording, viewing their own performance, and noting improvements in their teaching competencies. Continuous assessment of student performance is done through four assignments, one every month, each based on four to five study units. Formal examination is conducted at the end of the semester. Evaluation of the different programme components is done upon programme completion.

As of 1996, the programme had provided in-service training to more than 30,000 out of the target population of 42,000 primary school teachers. On the average, 62% of these students have completed the programme in all aspects except final examination. To determine programme effectiveness, five research studies have been conducted.

The programme is cost-effective. It offers the 18-week in-service teacher training at the cost of Rs.2300 (US $60) per student. Byproducts of the programme include the trained human resources: tutors, senior tutors, pretesters, evaluators, monitors, camera operators and technicians, and teacher trainers. The new PTOC has also provided study materials that have become assets for other teacher training programmes in the country. The main innovations of the new PTOC are:

— the use of media (print and electronic); outreach (emphasis on female teachers and rural teachers);

— developing teaching competencies by practical work;

— microteaching and the use of video cameras; non-formal and distance education mode;

— self-study materials with all the qualities of the distance education system;

— stress on change in teacher behaviour; incentives; strict monitoring system;

— face-to-face components (i.e., tutorials and workshops) within the non-formal education system;

— feedback system and programme evaluation for continuous improvement of the study materials.

The new PTOC is able to provide in-service teacher training to the bulk of primary school teachers at a very low cost. With its practical inputs, efficient methodology, innovative strategies, and encouraging results, PTOC stands as a good model for replication in Pakistan and other E-9 countries.

## In service Training Programmes

The in-service teacher training programmes reflect successful and innovative practices best suited to their respective contexts and circumstances. Orientation is defined as "a set of ideas about the goals of teacher preparation and the means for achieving them". Through their strategies and activities, the programmes represent varied viewpoints about the teaching-learning process and theories about learning to teach. Some of them, however, illustrate more than one perspective. This is to be expected inasmuch as the conceptual orientations are not mutually exclusive.

Academic Orientation sees teaching as being primarily concerned with transmitting knowledge and developing understanding. It stresses the role of the teacher as "intellectual leader, scholar, and subject-matter specialist".

The academic orientation is reflected in Brazil's training courses given by the Municipal Board of Education and Culture (SMEC) of Ijuí in partnership with the local university, UNIJUÍ. These courses seek to renew the teachers' knowledge in content areas and enable them to study theories about the learning process. It is likewise seen in Egypt's program to upgrade elementary stage teachers to university level, which includes general and specialization courses.

Indonesia's radio in-service training for primary school teachers is another example, given its aim of improving the teachers' mastery of subject matter content.

The practical orientation is exemplified in the sub-cluster training programme of Bangladesh, wherein teachers are exposed to demonstration lessons and modules on specific problems and issues about classroom teaching and school management, and are given opportunities to discuss and share experiences about these.

Mexico's programme on attitude and concept formation (IACAE) uses action research methodology to help teachers develop teaching competencies. Nigeria's Peer In-Service Approach (PISA), for its part, uses the pragmatic method of tapping the expertise of good teachers in some schools to help improve the teaching skills of teachers in other schools within the vicinity. For the Primary Teacher Orientation Course (PTOC) of Pakistan, experienced tutors and senior tutors provide guidance to the teacher trainees.

Technological Orientation, which concentrates on the knowledge and skills of teaching, aims primarily to develop proficient teachers who are able to demonstrate the application of principles and practices obtained from the formal study of teaching. It appears to be common to the selected training programmes in the E-9 countries.

The Bangladesh programme, for example, aims to help primary school teachers improve and update techniques appropriate for different teaching-learning situations and to strengthen their capacity to apply teaching techniques effectively. The training courses of the SMEC-UNIJUÍ partnership in Brazil likewise seek to provide teachers opportunities to study theories about the learning process and to conceive more dynamic and creative teaching strategies that would help enliven classroom lessons. The content of the in-service teacher training in China also includes educational theories, curriculum and pedagogy, educational practice, and basic teaching skills.

Similarly, Egypt's programme is directed toward improving teacher's abilities and skills to teach, manage, and effectively participate in classroom and school activities. In India, participants in the Certificate in

Guidance (CIG) programme are enabled to take theory-based preventive measures to overcome learning and socio-emotional problems of elementary school children. The radio in-service programme of Indonesia also attempts to upgrade the primary school teachers' instructional competencies. And in Pakistan, a major component of its PTOC is the development of eight specific teaching competencies through microteaching.

Personal Orientation puts the teacher-learner at the core of the educational process. "Learning to teach is construed as a process of learning to understand, develop, and use oneself effectively". Thus, the personal development of the teacher forms a central part of teacher training.

In Brazil, the SMEC-UNIJUÍ partnership's goal is to increase the rural teachers' self-esteem and credibility by helping them become agents and authors of their practice. In China, the stated purpose of continuing education given by teacher training schools is to improve the teachers' professional ethics and teaching capacity, and enable them to develop professional qualities based on their own current levels.

India's CIG programme likewise illustrates the personal orientation, with its objective of helping teachers (as well as parents) understand their role in guiding the elementary school children, in light of the growth and development process. Mexico's IACAE endeavours to give back to teachers their importance as a principal part of their students' cultural, political, and social life. The activities therefore seek to foster attitude change and enhance self-esteem. Nigeria's PISA, on the other hand, in its choice of "itinerant in-service teachers," focuses on the crucial contribution of peers as role models.

In China, the State Education Committee (SEDC) taps teacher training schools as the major channel and base for performing the mission of continuing education and for ensuring its quality and effectiveness. Likewise, in Egypt, the Ministry of Education cooperates with faculties of education. India's National Council of Educational Research and Training (NCERT) works in collaboration with the Indira Gandhi National Open University (IGNOU). Similarly, Indonesia's Open Learning University (Universitas Terbuka; UT) works hand in hand with the Centre for Communication Technology for Education and Culture (Pustekkom).

In Brazil, teachers bring their practices, questions and needs to the Education Board, where these topics are discussed and reflected upon, with the help of university professors. Later, the primary school teachers discuss the results of the board meeting and decide on new sets of action to be performed.

This back-and-forth process allows them to experimentally design their grade curriculum, set up goals and define basic concepts to be explored in each content area. A similar process is observed in Mexico, where self-evaluation is an integral part of the programme, and where monthly meetings are held to record and analyse problems and propose alternative solutions.

India's CIG programme requires that the trainees have a variety of interactions-with self-learning materials, with audiovisual materials, with their evaluators, with counsellors, teachers, and peers during contact programmes. Similar types of interactions are found in the sub-cluster training of Bangladesh, in the continuing education programmes conducted by the teacher training institutions in China, in Egypt's upgrading programme, and in Pakistan's PTOC.

## Microteaching Method

The distance-learning mode applied by Egypt, India, Indonesia, and Pakistan does not, however, preclude the teachers' personal contact with supervisors and/or peers. The self-learning activities required by the distance education programmes (in Egypt, India, Indonesia, and Pakistan) are supplemented by small-group learning activities.

On the other hand, the face-to- face formats of the in-service programmes in Bangladesh, Brazil, China, Mexico, and Nigeria are more appropriately designed for small-group learning. China, however, further utilizes large-group instruction by full-time trainers in town school classrooms. Mexico, in addition, employs a community learning approach through its community organization seminars. The programmes can also be classified according to the teacher education models they represent.

These are courses offered by universities and colleges and "include conversion courses for the purpose of upgrading qualifications, a wide variety of specialist graduate diplomas ..., the in-service B.Ed. degree, and masters degree in education". Programmes offering such courses are those of Egypt (awarding BA or BSc), India (CIG), and Indonesia (80 credits).

Although many counties and city districts in China offer special funds for in-service teacher training, many teacher training schools are experiencing financial difficulties with respect to their new training task.

## Teacher Education and Distance Learning

The Dakar conference revealed that there were still more than 100 million children out of school: they need teachers as the world moves towards the 2015 target of education for all. And we need to raise the skills of the existing 60 million teachers, too many of whom are untrained and unqualified. Beyond that, the skills and knowledge all teachers need are no longer fixed and familiar targets but moving ones.

Teachers therefore need more opportunities than ever before to go on learning throughout their careers. One of the ways of strengthening the teaching profession is to use distance education or open and distance learning.

Many countries still do not have enough teachers. In some, the expansion needed in the teaching force is far beyond the capacity of traditional colleges. The supply of teachers is also adversely affected in countries where retention rates are low for newly trained teachers or where significant numbers of teachers are being lost through HIV-AIDS or in rural areas which have difficulties in recruiting and retaining teachers. Teacher quality is an issue in most countries.

Many teachers are untrained or underqualified or teaching subjects in which they are not qualified or trained. In addition, teachers face a widening range of demands and roles. National governments, international organisations and specific circumstances continually set new goals:

— gender parity by 2005 and universal basic education by 2015;

— inclusive education;

— education for democracy, peace and social cohesion;

— multi-grade teaching;

— increased accountability for achieving learning targets;

— the development of learners who are self-managing and independent, skilled in critical thinking and problem solving, equipped with life-skills;

— the preparation of learners who are competent for knowledge-based economies, capable in the use of information technology; and

— the expansion of teachers' roles to include social work in communities where child-headed households and orphans are common as a result of HIV-AIDS.

The attention given to teacher education and their continuing professional development has in many cases lagged behind that given to other parts of the education system. Some countries lack a policy for it, though the importance of teachers is emphasised in many international reports.

Although there is wide recognition that teacher education, training and professional development need to be integrated, in ways that operationalise lifelong learning for teachers, the resources allocated to it are usually inadequate and the opportunities too few. In some countries teachers can expect one week's in-service professional development once every five to ten years.

On average, countries spend around one per cent of their annual education expenditure on the continuing professional development of teachers. All of this creates new challenges for teacher education and continuing professional development: the need to find ways of using existing resources differently, of expanding access to learning opportunities at affordable cost, of providing alternative pathways to initial teacher training, of drawing on new constituencies of the population to work as teachers, of using technologies appropriately to enrich a teachers' context and support practice, of stimulating and supporting teachers' active learning and of reconceptualising the traditional organisation of initial teacher education and continuing development.

Some countries have used distance education to provide a route to initial qualifications for significant numbers of teachers, both new entrants to teaching and experienced unqualified teachers. Distance education is therefore also being used to raise the skills, deepen the understanding and extend the knowledge of teachers. Some programmes are broadly focused while others are targeted at specialist groups. Programmes are taken either by individuals or by groups of teachers who are encouraged to participate by their schools or their employers.

Distance education has been used for teachers' career development. As they seek promotion, or aim for the next qualification level, or aspire to become a headteacher, or work in a teachers' college, or become an inspector, teachers need to acquire new skills. A multinational distance education project in West Africa has developed a training programme in school management for headteachers and aspiring heads. These categories inevitably overlap: career development may be regarded as part of continuing professional development; it blurs a distinction between the initial education of new recruits to teaching and of experienced but unqualified teachers.

In general, distance education programmes have been developed with varied intentions: of widening access to teaching qualifications; of disseminating good practice; of strengthening the education system as a whole by reaching not only teachers but the wider community; in enabling school-based training and professional development and as a means of strengthening the links between theory and practice, focusing on the school as a site of teachers' learning.

Distance education been used to teach, support and develop teachers for many years: UNESCO was a pioneer through its UNRWA/UNESCO Institute of Education which was training teachers for refugees forty years ago. While the success of programmes has varied, experience demonstrates that distance education can be used to enable teachers to learn and to gain qualifications.

The use of new information and communication technologies has drawn new attention to open and distance learning and offers new possibilities. Distance education has been defined as an educational process in which a significant proportion of the teaching is conducted by someone removed in space and/or time from the learner.

Open learning, in turn, is an organised educational activity, based on the use of teaching materials, in which constraints on study are minimised in terms either of access, or of time and place, pace, method of study, or any combination of these. The term 'open and distance learning' is used as an umbrella term to cover educational approaches of this kind that reach teachers in their schools, provide learning resources for them, or enable them to qualify without attending college in person, or open up new opportunities for keeping up to date no matter where or when they want to study.

The flexibility inherent in open and distance learning, and the fact that it can be combined with a full or near full-time job, makes it particularly appropriate for the often widely-distributed force of teachers and school managers. Some open and distance learning programmes lead to a qualification, others do not; some are addressed to individuals and others to groups; some are tightly organised and others essentially a way of making learning resources available to teachers.

## Developing Primary Teachers' Knowledge and Skills in Child Guidance, India: A Case Study

This case describes a programme in Child Guidance for primary teachers, parents and social workers, provided by the Indira Gandhi National Open University (IGNOU) in India. Using printed text, audio and video materials it provides a practically-oriented non-specialist programme which is not otherwise available. The numbers of students have been relatively small.

### *The context*

Though the study of child development and guidance has become a low priority subject in education in India, the need for it is increasingly recognised by teachers and parents. It is included in teacher education pre-service programmes and a small number of postgraduate ones of a theoretical nature, but easily accessible, basic level programmes of a practical nature were lacking.

A perceived need for one by individual staff at the National Council of Educational Research and Training (NCERT) and some parent-teacher associations led to the development of the Certificate in Guidance. This was produced through a collaboration between NCERT and the Indira Gandhi National Open University (IGNOU), the apex distance teaching university in India). NCERT developed the curriculum, content and materials, first in English, then in Hindi, and IGNOU ran the programme.

## *The programme*

The Certificate in Guidance programme aims to extend understanding about child development (ages 5-11) and to suggest practical strategies to facilitate children's all-round development. It takes about 480 hours of study over six months but students can extend this to two years. The four constituent courses are provided in two languages, Hindi and English (a limitation for speakers of other Indian languages).

Printed materials (nine booklets) are supplemented by five audio-cassette and four videocassettes. Twelve optional face-to-face tutor-led meetings are provided at weekends at local study centres. Students complete two assignments of a practical nature per course (a total of eight) and sit an examination. On successful completion they are awarded a Certificate in Guidance by IGNOU.

*Table 1*

| | |
|---|---|
| Population (millions) | 992.7 |
| Size ('000 km 2 ) | 3,288 |
| GDP per capita (purchasing power parity US$) | 2,248 |

| | | |
|---|---|---|
| Human Development Index | | 0.571 |
| Educational data | Primary | Secondary |
| Teaching force total '000 | 1,789,733 | – |
| '000 female | 584,953 | – |
| Gross enrolment ratio | | |
| All students | 100 | 49 |
| Female | 90 | 39 |
| Pupil teacher ratio | 47 | 33 |

Source: UNDP 2001; UNESCO 2000; UNESCO 2001

Note. Population, Size, GDP, and HDI figures are for 1999; Education figures are 1996

### *Media and technology*

IGNOU is equipped to use a variety of media and technology (radio and television, audio-teleconferencing, audio- and videocassettes, phone-in radio programmes and print). However, for the Certificate in Guidance programme, appropriate technology choices were print, audio- and videocassettes (low cost to produce and use, accessible by students).

Print materials were the main medium for the programme and, for some students, the only one they used. Print alone was available in the early years of the programme and audio-and videocassettes were added later as supplementary material. The videocassettes are available at local study centres for viewing there, usually during the tutor-led sessions. In practice, a low level of use of audio and video materials is reported, mainly because of low student attendance at study-centre sessions. The materials have had no revision since their production in 1993 and some students have found the level of language difficult.

### *Funding and costs*

The development costs of print (borne by NCERT) are estimated to be US $10,000 in 1993. Programme delivery (including print costs, tutorial support, distribution, examinations and administration) is funded by IGNOU. The Certificate programme is a small half-year programme out of a total of about 50 larger and longer programmes provided by IGNOU and cost data on it is limited and difficult to disentangle from other IGNOU programmes and services. The cost per successful student is not available but the total cost per enrolled student is about US $76. The costs of learning materials per enrolled student are about US $3 for printing the booklets, US $10 for developing them, and US $4 for the set of audio and video materials.

Teaching costs (tutoring and study centre facilities) are US $36. Because of the low numbers, the Certificate programme costs more per student in teaching costs than other IGNOU programmes. Fees charged to students are Rs.500 (the equivalent of US $16 in 1993 and US $10 in 2001). Other costs borne by students are between US $12 and US $24, an affordable sum for primary teachers (whose salary is around US $1,800 a year) or for middle-class mothers but not for those with lower incomes. Like other short-term updating or refresher programmes for teachers, the Certificate does not attract any financial increment to a teacher's salary.

### *Quality, effectiveness and outcomes*

The programme is regarded by the providers (NCERT and IGNOU) as a good one, with high quality curriculum, assignment design and printed materials (purchased by those outside the programme too). It has been able to take advantage of its location in a large distance teaching university and the services and resources that this can offer. The providers see the programme as serving a useful social purpose and meeting needs otherwise neglected.

However, they are also concerned at the relatively small numbers enrolling (less than a thousand each year) and low completion rates. Between 1993 and 2001 a total of 6,546 students enrolled for the programme (an average of about 700 students a year). Of the 5,659 students enrolling between 1993 and 2000, 887 (15.7 per cent) have successfully completed it. One reason for this appears to be the heavy study demands of the programme which is constrained by the assessment requirements of a credited course.

The question of whether or not a course of this kind should be examined and accredited has been debated by the providers. Other reasons identified include weaknesses in the learner support provided, a need for simpler language in the study materials and speedier feedback to students on their written work, and the heavy workload involved. No evaluation has been done of the impact of the programme on teachers' work in schools. The programme has attracted more women than men: 68 per cent female and 32 per cent male for students enrolling 1999-2001; 15 per cent of students come from Deprived Sections of Society (according to the Government's classification; 50 per cent of places in educational institutions are reserved for Deprived Sections as affirmative action).

Major problems in curriculum reform and change have been informing teachers in time, involving them sufficiently in the change process and supporting them as they change their beliefs and practices either as individuals or groups. This is frequently neglected. Solutions have often resulted in slow information flows, inadequate or scarce support materials and slow, expensive cascades of increasingly diluted information with insufficient support for applying new approaches and practices in teaching.

### *ICT and teacher education*

ICT in teacher education refers to two sets of activities or roles. One is training teachers to learn about ICT and its use in teaching as computers are introduced to schools. In many countries this is being done through face-to-face training programmes, often as part of initial teacher education.

Some countries have developed policies which require all initial teacher education programmes to include compulsory courses in ICT as a strategy for building capacity in ICT. In other countries, no policy yet exists and teaching teachers about ICT is at best an option within teacher education programmes.

In some cases, the facilities and equipment for supporting a strong policy are inadequate. The other role of ICT is as a means of providing teacher education, either as a core or main component of a programme, or playing a supplementary role within it.

There are many examples to be found of ICT forming part of a conventional programme of initial teacher education and whether this is a compulsory or optional part depends on government policy in a country. Sometimes this is taught as an on-campus subject or in some cases it can be taken in an alternative distance learning mode. There were far fewer examples to be found of ICT as a core means of delivering or supporting initial teacher education programmes, especially in developing countries.

There were more examples of online use for continuing professional development programmes at diplomas and higher degree level and for short courses. A great deal of activity is to be found at present in the use of ICT in providing informal professional development for teachers through online activities ('chat rooms', specialist subject conferences, virtual classrooms, networks, professional development websites, peer group discussions, bulletin boards, resource sharing). This gives teachers access to people and resources as well as putting more choices for professional development (formal and informal) into teachers' hands.

The advantages of ICT lie in its potential for increased interaction with and between learners, speedier delivery and response times to queries and feedback on assignments, greater access to communities of teachers and quicker lead-in times for updating course materials while at the same time needing the establishment of effective quality assurance procedures. The use of ICT and CD-Roms, is becoming more common for materials developers of distance education programmes of all kinds and for supporting administrative processes and staff involved in tutoring or learner-support.

Distance education programmes are provided through a variety of organisational arrangements. Some are located in universities or institutions, some are provided through consortia or collaborations, and others are time-limited projects, often donor-funded. One programme is provided by a distance teaching teachers' college. Three are donor-funded projects and one more is a programme provided by a consortium of private agencies, managed by the philanthropic division of a commercial, national communications network and privately funded.

Distance teaching universities may also have inflexible requirements as a way of ensuring standards. As a result, they may have inappropriate requirements for some non-formal programmes. In addition, teacher education programmes often involve partnerships: with schools, local education officers, teachers' colleges, school inspectors, headteachers and district authorities.

## Community Telecentres and Lifelong Learning

In informal education—the world of learning that goes on informally all around us—information and communication technology (ICT) is causing quite a stir, sometimes in the most unlikely of places. In developing countries on every continent, public ICT access centers are springing up and bringing information from around the world to communities that, for the most part, have had little experience with it. The phenomenon is particularly interesting in poor neighborhoods and remote and rural areas, where formal schooling suffers from access, equity, and quality problems and where, heretofore, informal opportunities for learning have been more or less limited to local wisdom. Though the experience varies from place to place, these centers are emerging as a new learning system for people of all ages and from all walks of life. Known by a variety of names, but generically as telecenters, they represent a potential means to enable lifelong learning in the best and broadest sense of the notion. Yet, unequal access to ICT—also known as the digital divide—is an increasingly important concern in international development and education communities. While computers are spreading at a faster rate than any other technology in history, the gap between those with access and those without is growing as well.

Less than 5% of computers connected to the Internet are in low-income countries, where fewer than four telephones per hundred people is the norm. Nearly half the world's population has never even made a telephone call. And a computer alone, much less a telephone line that enables Internet connectivity, is an unattainable goal for most people in developing countries.

The most literal definition of access is to make Internet, computing, and telecommunications tools available in a given community. Once the technical issues are solved, those who already understand the advantages of ICT—a relatively small segment of the population—will use it. In this model, entry and start-up costs are relatively low. The risk, however, is that the digital divide within countries will widen. Adding orientation and demonstration programs to the process combines access with awareness. This approach takes time, money, and planning, but it reaches beyond the technical elite to other early adopters who, given the opportunity, will take the time to learn and take advantage of the potential educational benefits of ICT. The most comprehensive approach to a full-bodied access program includes diffusion, which involves a preplanned, systematic program of activities designed to spread the message broadly. Diffusion is time-consuming and resource-intensive, but it is how disadvantaged groups-those lacking access-are reached.

Effective diffusion programs focus on local needs and priorities, both in the message conveyed and the method used. What works in one environment may not work in another. To exploit the potential benefits of ICT for widespread lifelong learning, therefore, ICT access involves more than making equipment available, though that, too, is important. The full complement of access concerns includes:

— reliable hardware;

— appropriate software;

— awareness of ICT functions and benefits;

— effective training in use;

— equitable/affordable opportunities for use;

— sufficient literacy/language skills-or access to mediators;

— ability to synthesize, organize, and apply information; and

— ability to produce and disseminate information as well as receive it.

Public ICT access centers are diverse, varying in the clientele they serve and the services they provide. Some for-profit, private-sector cyber cafes cater to those able to pay well for online time, providing young people with a place to play computer games, for example, or talk in chat rooms. At the other end of the spectrum is the small computer kiosk, also a commercial endeavour but typically offering offline services only, for example, at outdoor country markets.

The version designed specifically to achieve education and development goals-including affordable access and training for students, teachers, nongovernmental organizations (NGOs), and other social development agents-is the most likely to ensure access for targeted, low-income populations. Sponsored, subsidized telecenters-initially supported by local or national governments, bilateral or multilateral donor agencies, private foundations, or local entrepreneurs—are a case in point. This type of telecenter typically offers a host of technology products and services, ranging from a telephone, photocopier, and fax machine to computers equipped with a variety of software and peripherals, such as a printer and scanner.

A place for public access to ICT, these telecenters often offer technical assistance and training in use at rates affordable for low-income people. They build on the concept of public access but emphasize the learning functions of the communication technologies that are made available, thereby increasing access to lifelong learning opportunities. To ensure relevance to community priorities, needs assessments are conducted to identify needed products and services, and telecenter staff are trained to help visitors become familiar with the technologies, resources, and services offered at the centers. To facilitate long-term sustainability, fee and management structures are established based on ability to pay, and community involvement, as well as collaboration with the private sector, are actively promoted.

Telecenters providing affordable IT access, training for disadvantaged communities, and access to resources and information for social development face fiscal sustainability issues. Global telecenter experience indicates useful approaches for achieving sustainability. As demonstrated in the examples above, these include:

— creative marketing to diverse groups to increase client use of ICT;

— sliding fee scales to enable access by low-income groups;

— subsidizing ICT use, at least initially, to create demand;

— offering training programs to create client capacity;

— launching creative alliances with public, private, and voluntary sector partners for inputs; and

— working with the private sector to launch ancillary, spin-off businesses and engage in e-commerce.

On the surface, there is no traditional, preconceived resistance to women using computers. Yet, research indicates that many factors mitigate against equitable access to ICT for women, and experience suggests that, even where access is available, the more sophisticated the technical task, the more men tend to dominate. In training courses, for example, women tend to enroll in word processing classes while men are more likely to take an introductory course in using the Internet. Experience also indicates that gender equity in the use of ICT will be achieved more easily with specific interventions, beginning with outreach and social marketing, that demonstrate how higher-order ICT processes can benefit women. Beyond that, larger issues related to "income, time, literacy, education, language, and culture affect access to facilities, training, and employment in the IT area." Despite frequent claims to the contrary, information technology is not gender neutral.

Though marketing still is needed to reach disadvantaged groups, there is growing demand for ICT access, training, and use among all sectors of society. Experience indicates that, among low-income people, disadvantaged populations, ethnic minorities, and rural and remote communities, there is growing awareness that ICT provides new opportunities—and new hope for breaking the cycle of poverty.

# 6

# Images of Teacher Education

The integration of ICTs into the very idea of teaching and learning might be termed the 'informatization ' of education. Informatization represents the necessary component, condition, and catalyst for the modernization of education, which will permit the move from the reproductive model of teaching and learning to an independent model that promotes initiation and creativity with information. This new model of education reinforces the role of independent research.

Learners are expected to collect, select, analyse, organize, and present knowledge. Teachers are expected to promote collective work and to facilitate individual and group activities. The implementation of this new model builds the information and communication competencies of students, including the habits of mastering the means of information and communication technologies.

The most important principle for the individual development of a teacher is active, project-based learning.

Teaching must be carried out in such a way as to strongly reflect the general principles of education, such as the implementation of an informatization programme.

In this way it is possible to describe and demonstrate vividly the essential elements, connections, processes, and mechanisms of ICT-based teacher education without being constrained by the peculiarities of local settings. The resulting scenarios are thus not documentary videos of actual events, but rather animated cartoons of what is advisable to take into account as a starting point toward further development. Each scenario includes a commonly accepted maxim or generic statement; an interpretation, explanatory description, and visual enactment; and implications.

Providing specific interpretations of a general notion is a powerful, simple, and easily understood method of explanation that helps the audience to become aware of what they may achieve on their own. The scenarios are compiled from the experts ' actual experience of more than fifteen years educating thousands of teachers in the former republics of the Soviet Union, in Central Europe and Latin America.

The process of teacher preparation, involving the use of documentary videos, as a promising model for teacher education, is described. The major participants in the process of teacher development and thus major "players" in this model are:

a) *Educational designers*: The role of an educational designer is to provide heuristic and conceptual support at those moments when an urgent and ill-defined problem presents itself to the teacher working alone.

b) *Professors*: The classic role of the professor has been significantly transformed. Rather than being the source of all information, at best a professor will only be able to trace the ever-accelerating ICT-related changes in education in general. It is unrealistic to suppose that after a year or two professors will become adroit users of even the basic ICT applications in teaching their subject matter. This means that for the systematic assimilation of such technologies, professors must get help from technologists.

c) *Technologists*: Technologists may be defined as follows:

— ICT-experienced colleagues in teacher education

— Professors of ICTs, highly competent, but rather less orientated to technology-related pedagogical perspectives

— Technical ICT experts and computer 'gurus', having no educational background

— Practising teachers competent in ICTs

— Student teachers competent in ICTs

— Schoolchildren competent in ICTs.

d) *Technical assistants.*

e) *Student Teachers* (both professionals enrolled for certification and undergraduates).

f) Pupils in schools in partnership with teacher education programmes.

One important form of professional development consists of visits to educational institutions that have varied experience using information technologies in teaching and learning. These visits may provide a range of interaction opportunities, from after-school discussions and apprenticeships to collaborative work or interaction with the whole educational ICT community.

The course also includes summarizing lectures and discussions ,where concepts, strategies, theoretical frameworks, and ideas put forward by the professor are reviewed and criticized by students, and sufficient time is devoted to giving detailed answers to students ' questions. All stages are recorded in detail. In this way, these lectures also become part of the project work. The results and outcomes of the project-based activities of each learning group include reflective analysis of the process of group work, and are used by students in further schoolwork and by the professors in their work with future student teachers.

Networked interaction between students, and professors, students and other Internet users locally, nationally, and globally begins during training and is continued after the teacher preparation course has ended. The main course site references the initiatives, results, and resources developed by activities of the previous student teachers in their educational systems, and provides information on the activities of their pupils.

Educational ICTs work most efficiently when used in solving problems that are important and interesting for students both in their private lives, and especially, in their learning activities. Thus we come to two 'streams ' of assimilation and mastery of ICTs in educating teachers. The first stream flows throughout general teaching courses, which encompass pedagogy, content, methods, and organization of the teaching and learning process. The second stream flows through separate modules in which ICT skills are mastered in a planned consecutive order and applied by the students to solve educationally relevant and personally interesting problems.

In this way the modular structure of ICTs emerges quite naturally. Every module, organized around a separate project, introduces students to a particular area of ICTs while developing their working capacities in other areas. Each stream is subdivided into an introductory activity and systematic teaching. These two elements, however, constantly overlap and enhance each other. This provides a basic model for a teaching and learning activity in school, although it may be modified and customized widely according to circumstances.

The aim of such projects is not only to help teachers learn specific pedagogical aspects of ICTs, but also to motivate them to use ICTs as tools to produce something useful and tangible that will enhance their teaching practices. In this process, the central figure is the student teacher, who is taught by the professor within the framework of the curriculum developed by the designer. The hope is that the activities used with the student teachers will eventually be used with their pupils.

In previous generations, and at least until the twentieth century, training teachers was a comprehensive task. Learners were organized in a pyramid, with each successive level representing a "better" learner. At the highest levels of the pyramid were the "best" learners, those who came through school with the best marks and could teach the others the content they had learned. They in turn were taught by professors who continued learning after school in order to learn more than the graduates. Today, rather than a pyramid, the model more closely resembles a circle.

Today's school tries to establish a real-world environment and make possible an approach in which knowledge does not pass from educational designers and text authors to professors, from professors to teachers, and from teachers to pupils. Rather it comes from all directions, and the roles of student, teacher and professor are interchangeable. In a successful ICT project all are co-learners, and students may very well support teachers, showing them how to use ICTs in their work.

The best path to learn how to use ICTs in teaching is to live, feel, think, and behave as if one were not only an adult teacher but also a pre-adolescent pupil. The adult professional is able to exploit previously accumulated wisdom, capacities for logical reasoning, and formal analysis to critically reflect on the very process of learning. To be able to assume both roles is quite an asset for an aspiring teacher. There are several diverse, often antagonistic philosophies, theories, and methods of education accepted and practiced in today's schooling.

Under particular circumstances each of these approaches may be appropriate, and we should not exclude any of them perfunctorily. After all, good teachers always make their own customized toolbox,an individually charted map, or a highly personal guidebook compiled from many sources and experiences.

Teachers may use ICTs in a variety of ways to support a traditional 'teacher-centred ' way of teaching,, such as drill and practice for memorizing facts and figures, or as automated tutorials to supplement teacher-controlled activities for particular pupils. Others may use ICTs to support a more pupil-centred approach, in which children conduct their own scientific inquiries or projects, often in collaborative groups, while the teacher assumes the role of facilitator or coach.

A good place to start is to ask an aspiring teacher to assume the role of a pupil who has an adult teacher who always stays beside her or him and is devoted exclusively to this pupil. The characteristics of this role include:

— A Teacher-Who-Always-Stays-Beside pays full attention to this pupil only

— A Teacher-Who-Always-Stays-Beside never leaves this one pupil for any other pupils in the classroom

— A Teacher-Who-Always-Stays-Beside learns the same new things (knowledge/skills) that the pupil learns

— A Teacher-Who-Stays-Beside is ready not only to help the pupil when s/he needs it, but to learn from the pupil as well.

Student teachers should investigate both roles. With this dual experience, they receive insight into how wonderful it would be to maintain similar relationships and exercise similar capacities in actual classroom practice.

The modern ICTs work well in such a model. They promise the unprecedented advantage of achieving more in less time and providing a more engaging and responsive learning environment with fewer negative physical and psychological factors. Behaviour, thinking, and content make up learning and teaching, at least as far as organized schooling is concerned.

Through design in the 'authentic ' reality of classroom practice these become accessible in two different ways. Behaviour is accessible through direct observation and recording. For example, new vistas and practical possibilities of observing objectively some important structural features and functional characteristics of the learner 's thinking are revealed when the computer is used as a 'thinking tool ' in various kinds of design, construction, cognitive-modelling, and problem-solving educational activities.

The digital portfolio may provide a record of educational events and activities of a student teacher. The contents may include classification, annotation, indexing, connections with digital materials used in learning, and the work of other student teachers. This portfolio may be used by the learner as well as by professors and future employers.

The faculty of a teacher training institution, or other group working on a teacher education programme, have different levels of competence in ICTs. There are members of the group who understand the value of ICTs in education and have the educational background and experience to be ready to lead a work experience element.

In teaching declarative knowledge one may use the traditional teacher-centred approach of lecturing or telling the students the information or concepts to be learned. The learning of declarative knowledge may be enhanced by the use of ICT tutorial or drill and practice programmes, gradually advancing in complexity. At this stage ICTs are not taught to or learned by the pupils.

There is no need for them as long as the instruction remains entirely teacher-controlled. Procedural knowledge, such as learning procedural rules may also be taught using ICTs in a totally teacher-controlled context. Noticeably better results, however, are achieved when control is given gradually to the pupil. In this case ICTs become subject matter to be taught and learned, if only partially and in subordinate status.

Student teachers have their first encounter with ICTs while experiencing the traditional lecture class approach. In this first stage, the teacher talks and the pupil listens and is supposed to memorize-and understand and appropriate-the material. By appropriate, we mean assimilate, acquire, make it one 's own intellectual possession, connect it more or less coherently to what is already known and assimilated, etc. Such appropriation may not automatically occur. It involves hard work by both the teacher and the pupil. Exposition has three sub-categories:

— *Memorization:* The pupil is expected to memorize the information the teacher gives out.

— *Interpretation:* The pupil must decide whether these words and phrases, which this dreary teacher utters, denote or connote something in extra-linguistic reality; the pupil must try to connect and relate them to something already known.

— *Valuation or envaluation:* The pupil must assign value to this information on a pragmatic level.

Pupils may try to increase understanding by such strategies as positioning themselves so that they see the teacher talking or sitting closer to watch the teacher 's face and gestures. When the teacher 's lecture is accompanied by visuals of main points addressed, it is also helpful to read silently the teacher 's words and phrases on the large screen.

To help student teachers to learn how ICTs can support a lesson of this kind, we ask the students to assume the role of a first grade learner. We can divide the student teachers into four groups and locate the groups in separate rooms. Each group is exposed to a prerecorded three-minute lecture about the teaching and learning of reading and writing by first grade students. The lectures are presented by video on large screens. The versions differ in the types and amount of additional ICTs used to enhance the effect of the teacher 's speaking.

— *Version Zero*: The student teachers only hear the lecturing professor.

— *Version One*: The student teachers hear and see the lecturing professor.

— *Version Two*: The student teachers hear and see the lecturing professor along with the typed key words and short phrases of the speech appearing concurrently on the board.

— *Version Three*: The student teachers hear and see the lecturing professor, the key words/phrases, and related pictorial images appearing concurrently on the adjacent screen.

In all versions the student teachers hear a professor telling them the same content in absolutely identical wording and intonation. When the lecture is over, each student teacher is asked to repeat the lesson. It must be done twice: first alone, just for the video and soundtrack recording; then in the presence of a tutor who listens sympathetically, but remains silent and does not show any negative reaction.

The retellings by each student teacher are transcribed verbatim and printed out. The transcription needs time, and the student teachers use this break for training in typing or other tasks used in operating digital equipment. At the plenary session students are given a hardcopy of the original full text of the lecture and their retelling of it. The length of the retelling made in each group will be scored against the length of the original lecture, and the averages will be presented in numerical and graphic form on the large screen.

It is clearly shown that the length of retelling time increases with the addition of the image of the speaking lecturer, the visual presentation of the typed text, and, finally, the pictorial images. The student teachers are asked if they can explain this phenomenon, and we conduct a discussion, enabling everyone to gain the first insights into the great educational potential of ICTs. There is also a noticeable increase in the length of the retelling made in the presence of a sympathetic silent listener.

In ancient times mastery was inseparable from the sacred proto-technologies of shamanism and liturgical ceremonies, practised by truly wise men and women-masters in spiritual traditions. Unfortunately, as technological capabilities increased, this wisdom aspect of mastery became less important and was finally forced out by purely economic or military considerations.

Contemporary master teachers are called on to restore the dual meaning of mastery in its completeness. To achieve mastery, one must have significant procedural knowledge. The master demonstrates skill in the craft, and the apprentice, observing, begins to learn the craft, skill by skill. The apprentice gradually gains competency, and develops clusters of skills for performing definite tasks and knowledge of procedures.

The trouble is that genuine master teachers are scarce and accessible only to a chosen few. Each can mentor perhaps half a dozen apprentices, and, until very recently, the time-span needed for an aspiring apprentice to become equally knowledgeable and skilful in teaching inevitably stretched to many years, if not decades.

For the last two centuries, apprenticeship has been thought obsolete because it was totally incompatible with the machine, the epitome of industrialization. The post-industrial era prompts us to revise this view profoundly. ICTs offer new options for the apprenticeship model. Long sequences of events can be recorded and kept for posterity. It is easy to replay these sequences at full length or in part, selected for the closest and most meticulous scrutiny.

A student-apprentice can watch a master working from many points of view, around the clock, seven days a week if desired. It becomes possible to approach exemplar activities with learning strategies unthinkable in the past. The results promise to infinitely exceed, in relation to the time required, those achieved earlier through the natural capacities of the naked eye.

With ICTs, we can capture through video the best teaching practices of master teachers and share them with novice teachers. We can record electronically almost everything related to their joint teaching/learning activities. After collecting a sufficient amount of such material we can select, edit, and deliver these materials via multimedia CD-ROMs, DVDs, and WWW to any number of novice teachers applying for apprenticeship. Every one of them would undoubtedly gain much first-rate information and knowledge of how each master teacher uses ICTs in education.

During the Introductory Course, the student teachers are shown a number of recorded scenes in which schoolteachers and schoolchildren use ICTs in various ways. They are asked to: l) Describe, interpret, and explain what they have heard and seen m) Make corresponding conceptual constructs n) Compose a summing-up essay with the help of the word-processor and the graphic editor.

The student teachers have enough elementary ICT knowledge and skills to work at the level of first-graders. The difference in their task from that of the first-graders is that the focus of their presentation must be an analytic/synthetic survey of the ICT-assisted teacher/pupil communication/interaction, however technically simplistic and naive.

Each student teacher's action-adding, changing, or deleting an element-is saved automatically and filed separately as a numbered draft with an indication of which alphanumeric, graphic, or video sample from the sample-pool has been used and stored in the student teacher 's portfolio.

The multimedia presentation given at the end of the introductory term serves as a point of departure and reference for further development of the student teacher. The latter part of the portfolio includes recordings of the student teacher 's performance in the role of a teacher giving classes at the affiliated experimental school, with an indication which samples were chosen and used for imitation and modelling. These will be used for evaluation of the student teacher 's progress.

Some of the professors will use ICTs extensively in their work and may be ready to provide a comprehensive array of technology-based learning resources to students. Some will ask a technology specialist to provide a few hours ' technical training and will give students independent work in the course.

During the courses the student teachers use various models of ICTs in teaching and learning activities. During their student teaching activities, they will further reflect on the theoretical and practical elements of ICTs. When these students become teachers, they will apply in the classroom what they have learned and use with their own students the activities they have experienced. These activities include the following:

— *Hypermedia Composition*: Compositions of this kind function as teachers' homework before their exposition of the lesson material in a classroom. After being deployed on the local network and then on the Internet, compositions can be used by other teachers and students in their own teaching and learning activities.

— *Multimedia Presentation*: Pupils' presentations provide the opportunity to develop the communicative dimension of information competence. Instrumental support of textual theses, quotations, visual images, and sounds help organize more succinctly the thoughts and speech delivery of all students, even those who would, in other circumstances, need extensive scaffolding by the instructor in order to succeed.

— *Project and Process Design*: Central to the model is the creation by the student of teaching objects and/or processes. It is important to remember the diverse ways in which these can be realized.

A computer can be downloaded with a great number and variety of exercises on arithmetic, grammar, completion tasks, etc. This makes it possible to assess in many ways, and to increase the efficiency of work of both teachers and students. When such testing is conducted in a computer lab, the teacher and students may receive the results immediately.

Computer-based testing, however, has many limitations, and the teacher must understand the limitations. Including such instruction in the teacher education programme may be very beneficial. ICTs make it possible to compensate for even serious deficiencies of the sense organs and supporting-motor apparatus. In cases of deaf and hearing-impaired, as well as blind and sight-impaired children, ICTs are used to enhance the functioning of a weakened organ, or to substitute for an inoperative one.

For children with disrupted kinetic functions, even as serious as cerebral paralysis, ICTs provide the possibility of communicating and interacting by means of text input and manipulation of screen objects. During the teacher-training course such situations can be simulated by artificial restrictions of movement, low lighting, etc.

An important emotional-motivational factor is offered by visiting a special educational institution, where ICTs are used to provide handicapped children access to learning and skills for future professional work in ICT environments.

The global network of the Internet makes possible individual contacts, communication, and interaction by student teachers with scientists and experts. There are thematic sites and specialized virtual conferences that facilitate intensive exchange and consultation on a wide range of topics.

A search on the Internet, encouraged by the professor and stimulated by the overall environment, may become a constant and habitual activity for a teacher. During the course the student teachers often refer to their recent findings on the Internet, which they transform into new tasks for pupils, or themes for academic competitions.

When ICTs are used extensively in the teacher education programme, there are extensive opportunities for research. Students may engage in recording, analysing, and reflecting on teaching objects and projects. The student teachers thus become reflective practitioners, who understand both the value and the methods of educational research.

In the year 1997, in India, New Delhi from February 6-8, a meeting of E-9 countries, the high population countries in the world, was held. One of the major purposes of the meeting was to share information on learning in grades 1 to 3, in particular reading, writing, and arithmetic, in the respective E-9 countries. The focus on learning has its roots in the World Conference on Education for All (EFA) held in Jomtien, Thailand in March 1990.

The UNESCO/UNICEF Monitoring of Learning Achievement Project (MLA), initiated in 1994 and involving 10 countries, including three E-9 countries (Brazil, China, Nigeria) is based on the premise that a systematic mechanism for monitoring student learning is essential to the improvement of the quality of basic education.

The assessment of the level of competence in the basic skill areas-literacy, numeracy and life skills-provides benchmarks against which progress in learning achievement can be determined as well as pointing the way for short-term and longer-term interventions.

At national level, the MLA project aims to establish and sustain a monitoring culture through capacity building to improve the performance of the educational system. The MLA project allows for the collection of information on important contextual variables such as textbook availability, sufficient instructional time, amount of homework and adequacy of instructional material and as such may be used to explain and to predict levels of competence in the various skill areas.

The E-9 meeting in New Delhi was informed by country-specific studies that described the syllabi for the 3Rs, textbooks and other learning materials; instructional time; student-teacher ratios, teacher qualifications, supervision of teachers, methods used in teaching, and technical input from international organizations.

Similarities and differences among E-9 countries, whether in curriculum, textbook production, instructional hours by subject, or teacher training requirements provide an enormous opportunity to learn from one another. The meeting in New Delhi opened the possibility of much more intensive interchange on topics of mutual concern to the E-9 countries.

At the meeting in Bali (Indonesia) in September 1995, the E-9 countries (Bangladesh, Brazil, China, Egypt, India, Indonesia, Mexico, Nigeria and Pakistan) decided to intensify inter-country activities to learn more from each other and exchange experiences on common concerns in the field of basic education. One of the areas identified for this exchange of information was teaching and learning the three core subjects of basic education: language (reading and writing) and mathematics. It was decided to conduct country studies to share information on acquisition of skills and knowledge in grades 1-3 in the respective E-9 countries.

*Table 1*
*Teacher qualifications and supervision in selected E-9 countries*

| Country | Requirements | Supervision |
|---|---|---|
| Brazil | Fundamental Education (8 years), plus 3 years of teacher training at a Normal School | evaluation conducted once a year |
| China | Specialised Normal Secondary Education | evaluation conducted once a year |
| Egypt | faculties of Education: (a) Basic Education Department or (b) Education for Special Purposes. Institutes: five years after preparatory certificate | Supervised a minimum of three times a year; end of. year evaluation includes principal of school |
| India | With some exceptions, two years pre-service is required, following ten or twelve years of general education; about 10% to 12% of primary teachers are untrained; states moving toward a two year diploma following twelve years of general schooling | state-specific veraition |
| Mexico | After 9th grade completion, study for four years (eight semesters) or a total of thirteen years | |
| Nigeria | Almost 32% unqualified. Grade two Teacher Certificate required; nine years of education required for entry to teacher colleges or twelve years to become a teacher: proposed changes would increase time to fifteen years | minimal inspection and supervision out of 38,000 schools only 600 visited in 1994; some rural schools |

| | | |
|---|---|---|
| | | not visited |
| Pakistan | Department of Public Instruction in Punjab Province and wings of Provincial Education Departments (PEDs) in the other three provinces recruit (from grade IO), select, train, certify primary level teachers-eleven years to become a primary teacher: pre-service curriculum over-loaded and too short (39 weeks-33 hrs per week-10 subjects) crisis regarding supply of teachers in general and particularly teacher quality (20% of male teachers and 26% of female teachers untrained); goal is to recruit more female teachers | |

Source: Based on E-9 country reports, UNESCO, 1996

In E-9 countries, characterised by great ethnic and cultural diversity, the language of instruction in the early grades is the mother tongue and/or regional language. Language of instruction is of particular importance with regard to the availability and competence of teachers to teach the curriculum in different languages. Nigeria is an example where the lack of adequate time and resources for the study of regional languages is a serious issue, although the language policy, which started in 1985, is innovative.

The allocation of time for different subjects relates to the curriculum's priorities and the curriculum's "balance." Ideally, there should be a balance between the courses required in the basic skill areas, such as language and mathematics, and non-academic subjects, such as art, music, and physical education. Curriculum balance can be assessed in terms of whether it addresses the cognitive, affective, and psychomotor needs of the primary age child.

The definition of what constitutes a qualified and trained primary teacher, with respect to pre-service, varies according to country, as can be seen. Further delineation of those terms awaits country-specific studies regarding both pre-service and in-service training to prepare competent and motivated teachers.

# Bibliography


Cuban, *Oversold and Underused: Computers in the Classroom*, London:Harvard University Press, 2001.

Becker, H. J. "How Exemplary Computer-Using Teachers Differ from Other Teachers: Implications for Realizing the Potential of Computers in Schools." *Journal of Research on Computing in Education*, 25, 291-320., 1994.

______________ ., "Teaching With and About Computers in Secondary Schools." *Communications of the ACM*, 36, 69-73. 1993.

Bitter, G. G. & Yohe, R. L., "Preparing teachers for the information age", *Educational Technology*,29 (3), 22-25, 1989.

Digumarti Bhaskara Rao, (ed.), *Teacher Training in Science and Technology Education*, Discovery, New Delhi. 2001.

Fox, *Successful ICT Leadership in Primary Schools, Learning Matters*. Due out in Autumn 2003.

G. Rasool, *Teacher Education*, Jammu, Vinod Pub., 2001.

J.S. Rajput and K. Walia, *Teacher Education in India*, New Delhi, Sterling, 2002.

Kulik, J. A. and Kulik, C-L., "Effectiveness of Computer- based Instruction." *School Library Media Quarterly*, 17, 156-159, 1989.

Maitreya Balsara, *Administration and Reorganisation of Teacher Education*, New Delhi, Kanishka, 2002.

Merrill,M.D "Constructivism and the Instructional Design" *Educational Technology* 31,no.5, pp.45-53, 1991.

Motteram, G., "Authoring tools and teacher training for CALL." *System*, 20/2 pp 151-160, 1992

Pachler, N. "Theories of Learning and ICT" ed. Marlyn Leask and Norbert Pachler. London: Routledge, 1999.

Pea, R. D & Gomez, LM "Distributed Multimedia Learning Environment, Why and How, Interactive Environment". 1992

R.P. Singh and Gopal Rana, (eds.), *Teacher Education in Turmoil : Quest for a Solution*, New Delhi, Sterling, 2002.

Riel, M & Fulton, K "Technology in the Classroom, Tools for Doing Things Differently or Doing Different Things", America Educational Research Association, San Diego. 1998

Savita Rastogi, *Teacher's Development in Higher Education*. New Delhi, Classical, 2001.

Stenhouse, L., *An Introduction to Curriculum Research and Development*. London: Heinemann, 1975.

Twining, 'Making Barriers Explicit: Some problems with the computer innovation literature', in Willis, Robins & Willis (eds), *Technology and Teacher Education Annual 1995*, pp.879-885, Association for the Advancement of Computing in Education, 1995.

Twining, "ICT and the nature of learning: implications for the design of a distance education course", in Paechter, Edwards, Harrison & Twining (Eds), *Learning, Space and Identify*, London: Paul Chapmen Publishing Ltd., 2001.

Twining, "IT into Education: A change effort worth pursuing?', in Willis, Price, McNeil, Robin & Willis (Eds), Technology and *Teacher Education Annual 1997* Volume 2, pp.1091-1094, Association for the Advancement of Computing in Education, 1997.

Twining, "Planning to use ICT in schools?", *Education* 3-13, Vol 29, Issue 1, pp.9-17, 2001.

US Department of Education. "An Educators's Guide to Evaluating the Use of Technology in Schools and Classrooms". December 1998.

# Index